M000028262

CONTENTS

Introduction 1

First Meditation – Acts 1:8 3

Second Meditation – Acts 1:15,16. 7

Third Meditation – Acts 2:1-6 11

Fourth Meditation – Acts 2:15-18. 17

Fifth Meditation – Acts 2:37-39, 42 21

Sixth Meditation – Acts 2:38 27

Seventh Meditation – Acts 3:6 31

Eighth Meditation – Acts 4:8. 35

Ninth Meditation – Acts 5:3 39

Tenth Meditation – Acts 5:19 43

Eleventh Meditation – Acts 6:3. 49

Twelfth Meditation – Acts 7:55 53

Thirteenth Meditation – Acts 8:24. 57

Fourteenth Meditation – Acts 8:39. 61

Fifteenth Meditation – Acts 9:17 65

Sixteenth Meditation – Acts 10:17-20 69

Seventeenth Meditation – Acts 10:44-47 73

Eighteenth Meditation – Acts 11:15-18 77

Nineteenth Meditation – Acts 13:2,3 81

Twentieth Meditation – Acts 13:9-11. 85

Twenty-First Meditation – Acts 13:52 89

Twenty-Second Meditation – Acts 14:17 93

Twenty-Third Meditation – Acts 15:28,29 97

Twenty-Fourth Meditation – Acts 15:36-41 101

Twenty-Fifth Meditation – Acts 16:6,7 105

Twenty-Sixth Meditation – Acts 16:14,15 109

Twenty-Seventh Meditation – Acts 16:16 115

Twenty-Eighth Meditation – Acts 17:16 119

Twenty-Ninth Meditation – Acts 18:1-4 123

Thirtieth Meditation – Acts 18:25 127

Thirty-First Meditation – Acts 19:10 131

Thirty-Second Meditation – Acts 20:7-12 135

Thirty-Third Meditation – Acts 20:22,23 139

Thirty-Fourth Meditation – Acts 21:10-13 143

Thirty-Fifth Meditation – Acts 21:37,38 147

Thirty-Sixth Meditation – Acts 23:11 151

Thirty-Seventh Meditation – Acts 26:27-29 155

Thirty-Eighth Meditation – Acts 28:25 159

Thirty-Ninth Meditation 163

Fortieth Meditation 169

Conclusion. 173

WHY WE NEED THE
HOLY SPIRIT

40 Days to a Deeper Encounter with the Holy Spirit

CHRIS PADGETT

little red house

PUBLISHING

Scripture passages are from the Revised Standard Version–Catholic Edition. Copyright © 1946, 1952, 1971, Division of Christian Education of the National Council of the Churches of Christ in the United States of America. All rights reserved.

Published by:
Little Red House Publishing
Tel: 941-704-3394
E-mail: chris@chrispadgett.com
Web: www.chrispadgett.com

Cover design and layout by Michael Fontecchio, catholicdesigner.com

ISBN: 978-0-9990211-0-1

Printed in the United States of America

DEDICATION

To my wife Linda.

INTRODUCTION

Many Catholics give the Holy Spirit little more than a cursory glance. We invoke him as we make the Sign of the Cross during the Mass and acknowledge him during the Creed, but do we really *know* him? Do we really *need* to know him? If so, *how* can we know him?

The title of this book promises a "forty-day encounter" with the Holy Spirit. But it is not a "how to" on speaking in tongues, nor is it a discourse on prophesy and the end times, nor is it a guide to give you ammunition to correct a family member or friend who is doing something wrong. It is not meant to foster warm feelings.

So who is the Holy Spirit? The Holy Spirit is the Third Person of the Trinity, the love of the Father and the Son, a divine Person who is a specific gift from the Father and the Son to you! The Holy Spirit is infinite power, but power that is always at the service of love. For "God is love" (1 John 4:8). The power we see in nature, such as the intensity of Niagara Falls, the destructive winds of a tornado or hurricane, or the shaking of an earthquake are only shadows of the strength of the Holy Spirit. While such disasters demonstrate nature's awesome power, they point to a power *beyond* nature, a power that is entirely "other." The Holy Spirit is beyond our ability to articulate or define, but we know that he is a loving divine *Person* who wants to change our life, destroy the sin within us, and breathe new beginnings into the old chapters of our story.

We are called to know the Spirit, especially in times of difficulty and need. This book contains forty brief meditations on the role of the Holy Spirit in our lives, with reflective questions at the end of each meditation for you to consider throughout your day. As you pray and reflect on these meditation and questions, it my firm belief that you will not only come to know more about the Holy Spirit of God but will begin to depend upon him and make him evident in your life.

Just as the Holy Spirit descended upon the early Church at Pentecost, enlivening and invigorating the followers of Christ to go and preach his resurrection, you too have been called to do the same through the power of the Spirit! With this in mind, we will use the Acts of the Apostle as a template to explore how the Spirit worked in the past, and how he continues to work in the lives of Christians today. Each meditation will explore a specific Scripture passage, give some basic catechetical teachings about the work of the Holy Spirit, and offer some practical application for how the Spirit works in and through us.

In this book, we show how the gifts of the Spirit given to you at baptism and strengthened at confirmation are meant to be applied at every moment of your day. These gifts—wisdom, understanding, knowledge, counsel, fortitude, piety, and fear of the Lord—help us to love and serve God and our neighbor. The more we reflect upon them and strive to live in them, the more we will be able to endure whatever happens in our lives. So the question isn't whether or not we need the Holy Spirit in our life but how can we build a relationship with him—the One who has sealed us in baptism, strengthened us in confirmation, and calls us to do amazing things for Christ in this life. Today is the day to begin understanding what it means to encounter and walk with the Holy Spirit!

First Meditation

"But you shall receive power when the Holy Spirit has come upon you; and you shall be my witnesses in Jerusalem and in all Judea and Samaria and to the end of the earth."

— Acts 1:8

Catechetical Application

How can you encounter the Holy Spirit through this passage?

What does it say about who the Holy Spirit is, what he does, and the gifts he gives?

I love how this passage mentions the connection of authentic power in evangelization with the Person and work of the Holy Spirit. God gives us what we need in order to do what he asks of us. Notice that Jerusalem, Judea, and Samaria are mentioned before the "ends of the earth." The clear implication, then, is that we should live the faith and apply the power of God's Spirit where we are first, and then seek to do so elsewhere. The saying, "Where God guides, he provides" applies here. The early Church got a glimpse into how the message of Jesus would reach the ends of the earth through the power of the Spirit when they "spoke in tongues" to the pilgrims in Jerusalem (Acts 2:4), allowing people of many nations to hear the Gospel preached in their own language.

PRACTICAL APPLICATION

How does this verse speak to you about your own life?

Make no mistake: you and I are meant to live out our love of Jesus Christ to those within our reach. We may not see the far reaching impact our faithfulness will have, but simply think about the reality that your children will one day grow old and live somewhere apart from you (in most cases). What will they be like and how will they act will largely reflect your faithfulness and commitment as a parent, on how well you taught them right from wrong and how to make wise decisions. You may raise your son on the East Coast, but he may end up living in California, where he will live in a manner that witnesses to your values.

We are all called to be missionaries, first to our families and friends, and then to those with whom we work and interact every day. Our missionary activity doesn't have to be a profound spiritual insight shared with a coworker; it can simply be a life well lived in Christ. In other words, we are missionaries simply by how we live. This reminds me of the well-known saying traditionally attributed to St. Francis of Assisi: "Preach the Gospel at all times ... when necessary, use words." As Catholics, we are called to live out our faith, to "bloom where we are planted," because the impact of a Christian willing to witness God's message of love and forgiveness is something our world desperately needs to see.

Remember that since God is working in and through you, the Holy Spirit will give you the strength to live in a way that makes a difference. In the passage from Acts quoted in this mediation, it is the Holy Spirit who "comes upon" us. So God is the initiator. This verse calls to mind the passage in Luke's Gospel when the Holy Spirit descended upon Mary at the Annunciation. When God speaks to Mary through the message

of an angel, her *fiat*—her unequivocal "yes" to God's will—results
in the Spirit of God descending upon her (Luke 1:35). This is
similar to how the Spirit descended upon Jesus in the form of a
dove when he was baptized by St. John the Baptist (Luke 3:22).
Interestingly, Luke is also the author of the Acts of the Apostles,
so the language he uses in these passages is intentional. He
wants to make sure that we understand that the same Spirit of
God who came upon Mary at the Annunciation and Jesus at his
baptism, affirming the mission of the Son, is the same Spirit who
is at work in our lives as well. That same Spirit who descended
upon the disciples at Pentecost empowers us to share our hearts
with others. There is a fluidity to the consistency of the Holy
Spirit, who does great things through small acts of openness. As
Christians, you and I are part of a great work—the work of the
Spirit in our willing hearts that can impact the lives of others.

Recently, I took a trip to Santa Barbara, California. While
there, I had breakfast with my friend John and a priest from
Africa. While we were waiting for our order, an older lady from
the parish at which I was speaking came over to talk to us. I
recalled meeting her on a previous visit. I learned that she was
fighting cancer, which was wreaking havoc on her body, but
she seemed happy despite her suffering. My wife, Linda, has
just begun a blog on happiness, and this woman mentioned
how much she loved the blog. Linda calls her blog, Linda360
(linda360.com), and posts articles about good food, family
"chaos" moments, marital insights, spiritual reflections, and
exercise tips. Since she doesn't travel as much as I do, she would
seemingly not be able to reach as many people as I can. Yet,
sitting in Santa Barbara I was able to find much comfort and
joy knowing that my wife's faithfulness in sharing the word
of God was touching the life of a woman dying from cancer on
the other side of the country. Of all the things she could read in
her final days, she chose to read the stories on my wife's blog.
This shows how, through the Holy Spirit, one person can be an

encouragement to another, even without the two knowing each other

What is the small act of faithfulness and willingness that you can say "yes" to today? The Holy Spirit is ready to empower you and work through you today. This action does not need to be some elaborate plan of how to evangelize the world. It can be something very simple, just "you being you" in the life of another. Your "yes" to the Holy Spirit will touch the lives of more people than you might imagine.

QUESTIONS

What is your Jerusalem?

How can you say "yes" to the Holy Spirit with your words and deeds?

praying for co-workers who have an illness or family member that is ill.

SECOND MEDITATION

"In those days Peter stood up among the brethren (the company of persons was in all about a hundred and twenty), and said, 'Brethren, the scripture had to be fulfilled, which the Holy Spirit spoke beforehand by the mouth of David, concerning Judas who was guide to those who arrested Jesus.'"

– Acts 1:15,16

CATECHETICAL APPLICATION

How can you encounter the Holy Spirit through this passage?

What does this Scripture say about who the Holy Spirit is, what he does, and what gifts he gives?

There is a lot of interesting information in this verse. First, we see that Peter is the primary voice in interpreting how the work of the Spirit fulfills the Scriptures. Vatican II's document on divine revelation, *Dei Verbum*, emphasizes this point by stating that it is the Church's Magisterium (the bishops in union with the pope) who is the primary interpreter of the Word of God, both in its written (Sacred Scripture) and oral (Sacred Tradition) forms. This passage shows us Peter, upon whom the Lord said he would build his Church (Matthew 16:18), interpreting a passage from the Psalms that David had written a thousand years earlier under the inspiration of the Holy Spirit. The word *inspiration* literally means, "breathed in"—God "breathed" his Spirit upon the authors of the Bible and inspired them to write only what he willed.

So in this brief passage from Acts we can see the authority of the Church (in the leadership of Peter), the divine inspiration of Scripture, the work of the Spirit through the words of David in the Psalms, and finally the message of hope amidst a great and seemingly devastating event—Judas' betrayal of Jesus. Remember, too, that Peter denied Jesus three times, but he had a profound moment of repentance; he did not give in to despair. Jesus reaffirms Peter's role at the end of John's Gospel: "Feed my sheep" (John 21:15-17). Jesus counters Peter's three-fold denial by a three-fold command to "tend" or "feed" his "sheep"—that is, the Church. Judas, though, after his betrayal did not allow the Lord to forgive and heal him, so he committed suicide. Judas' betrayal and death then left a vacancy in the original Twelve.

> For it is written in the book of Psalms, "Let his habitation become desolate, and let there be no one to live in it"; and "His office let another take." So one of the men who have accompanied us during all the time that the Lord Jesus went in and out among us, beginning from the baptism of John until the day when he was taken up from us-one of these men must become with us a witness to his resurrection.
> *– Acts 1:20-22*

So Matthias is chosen to fill Judas' place among the Twelve. But why not simply leave Judas' place vacant? Because Jesus established the office of the Twelve, so the apostles needed to choose a successor. Here we see the early Church maintaining the work and structure given it by Jesus, relying upon the Holy Spirit to ensure that God's will is being done faithfully.

Practical Application

What does this passage say to you about your own life?

There are always going to be moments in life when we feel as if all is lost, or when we are unable to see the light at the end of the tunnel. The early Church must have been devastated after the Lord's death, since they did not yet fully understand the promise he gave of his resurrection. So what were those three days like for his scattered followers? It would have been easy for the disciples to give in to despair. Yet the agony they felt on Good Friday quickly changes to joy in the Lord's resurrection. We too might encounter the betrayal or denial of a friend, but know that God is at work and can bring good from this evil.

We need to be aware that it is not against only "flesh and blood" that we struggle. Satan is always trying to persuade the faithful to abandon the mission of Christ and pursue the values of the world. Remember that Judas was one of the apostles Jesus himself chose, yet he ended up betraying the Lord. The Bible notes that Satan "entered into Judas" (John 13:27, Luke 22:3), so he played an active role in Judas' betrayal. As St. James promises, we will all encounter various trials, yet we must be willing to count them as joy (James 1:2). Why? Because God's work ultimately will not be hindered by the oppression of the enemy, nor by seemingly overwhelming circumstances, nor by the struggles we have with sin. How can we know that God is in control when we find ourselves in such moments of potential despair? Because he has given us a clear interpretive voice in the Church. We need to remember that Jesus gave Peter the commission to lead his Church and promised that the "gates of hell" would not prevail against it (Matthew 16:18). So we can not only be secure within the arms of the Church but also victorious over our struggles, sufferings, and doubts.

When you and I struggle with loss or even find ourselves broken from past events, do we seek comfort in the Church or in the Scriptures? The work that Jesus began in us at baptism is continued by the very Spirit we see in the Acts of the Apostles. The same Spirit who led the early Church will lead us in our decisions if as we lean upon him. We must not let loss and difficulties distract us from what God is calling us to. He has not left us orphaned, nor do things just "happen" to us randomly. The work of the Spirit in our lives is possible because God has willed for us to follow Jesus with our whole heart.

QUESTIONS

Do you struggle with difficult circumstances or past failings?

Can you see God working them for good?

What role does the Church have in your faith life?

Do you find comfort in reading the Scriptures? Why or why not?

Third Meditation

"When the day of Pentecost had come, they were all together in one place. And suddenly a sound came from heaven like the rush of a mighty wind, and it filled all the house where they were sitting. And there appeared to them tongues as of fire, distributed and resting on each one of them. And they were all filled with the Holy Spirit and began to speak in other tongues, as the Spirit gave them utterance. Now there were dwelling in Jerusalem Jews, devout men from every nation under heaven. And at this sound the multitude came together, and they were bewildered, because each one heard them speaking in his own language."
– Acts 2:1-6

Catechetical Application

How can you encounter the Holy Spirit through this passage?

What does it say about who the Holy Spirit is, what he does, and the gifts he gives?

This passage from Acts speaks of Pentecost, and it seems to be a counter of the classic story of language confusion at the Tower of Babel (Genesis 11:1-9). At Jesus' instruction, the disciples have been waiting for forty days for the Holy Spirit's— the "Consoler's"—promised arrival. They truly need consolation, given all that they suffered with Jesus during his passion. The Holy Spirit descends upon those gathered in the Upper Room, and they begin to utter the Gospel message in other tongues. Acts states that people from the surrounding nations began to hear the Gospel preaching in their own languages.

This moment is so profound for the early Church because the great longing to be united with God (they are all gathering in Jerusalem for worship) happens as they each hear the message of salvation in their own language. Instead of language dividing humanity—which had been the case since the Tower of Babel— the Spirit uses the preaching of the apostles to bring humanity together. What is an obstacle for human beings, communicating with one who speaks a different language, is not an obstacle for the Lord. This miraculous act of the Spirit working through "average" men—men who had failed miserably in their walk with Christ (e.g., they all fled at the garden, Peter denied Jesus three times, James and John argued over who was greatest, etc.)—is a profound witness and encouragement to us today. We too often doubt, struggle, and fall short in our faith lives, yet the Spirit enables us, even with our limitations, to speak the Gospel effectively to those who are not able to understand what we are saying.

Think about how often you are misunderstood or misunderstand others, even though you both speak the same language. What an amazing work of the Holy Spirit it was, then, for thousands to not only hear and understand the Gospel message in their own language but to then become Christians through baptism. The time of disunity was over, and in Christ the Spirit of God was present to bring people into this new universal family.

Since the Bible speaks of the Spirit as descending upon the disciples of Jesus as tongues of fire, I think it appropriate to reflect upon some other moments in Scripture when God "rains down fire." One example is the story of Sodom and Gomorrah (Genesis 19), cities that are so thoroughly evil that God announces to Abraham he will destroy them. Though they had every opportunity to repent, they had been so given over to sin that they could not hear God's message. In the end, only Abraham and his family are rescued, though Lot's wife "looks back" and turns into a pillar of salt.

Another example in the Bible of fire falling from heaven is the story of Elijah and the priests of Baal (1 Kings 18). Elijah calls upon the Lord to prove himself as the One true God, and he sets the stage for a "divine showdown." The altar is set, and the priests of Baal petition their god to rain down fire from heaven and consume the altar to prove his authenticity. All day they chant and petition, cutting themselves and crying out with no response. Elijah mocks them by asking if their god is sleeping. Then he does something quite extraordinary. He has them soak the wood of the altar with water to ensure that only a true miracle would ignite it. God then pours down fire from heaven and consumes the altar. The meaning of this fiery act is clear: the God of Israel is not to be ignored; there is none like him. The priests of Baal are destroyed and justice has been implemented through Elijah.

We can see how these stories are similar to Pentecost. The Spirit of God allows us to know the secret and deep things of God and to implement justice. Greater than a verdict upon the life or death of our mortal flesh, the speaker for God (those filled with the Spirit here) will implement justice, which has eternal ramifications. God is a consuming fire, and the Spirit coming upon the disciples in the Upper Room is a demonstration that the One true God is at work. The miracle of communicating with people of various languages also shows that the Holy Spirit is at work. While Sodom and Gomorrah were destroyed by God's fiery judgment, the fire of the Holy Spirit descends to save. Unlike the people of Sodom and Gomorrah, many in Jerusalem on Pentecost listen and believe. The Holy Spirit is a consuming fire, who comes to purifies and enable us to see—and live—the truth.

Practical Application

What does this passage say to you about your own life?

I have had the privilege of traveling to other countries, places where English is not the primary language. One such journey took me to the Netherlands, where a former student of mine had worked out an opportunity for my wife and I to come and speak for ten days to youth and adults at a church event. While Dutch was the native language of my audience, most had some understanding of English, having studied it in school and having watched many English-language movies and television programs. Nonetheless, this was my first presentation working with a translator. It was a bit distracting to speak, then pause for him to translate what I had just said into Dutch. My talks ended up twice as long, and many of my jokes and cultural references did not translate to my Dutch listeners. I was in a different land, with different customs and references, and we were clearly not speaking the same language, even when I had the translator hard at work putting my bizarre insights into their native tongue.

The cultural difficulty was even more evident when I spoke with the adults, many of whom had no understanding of English. I was entirely dependent upon my translator. It took me about half way through the first keynote to realize how I was in a collaborative relationship with my interpreter, and I saw that I would need to slow down and simplify my message. I quickly learned as much as I could about what they liked to eat, what music they listened to, and even how their education compared to that of the United States. Interestingly, the Dutch practice of eating bread and lunch meats for breakfast (very European) turned out to be a great comedic avenue for me. I emphasized my exhaustion at eating sandwiches for breakfast, which led them to ask me about what a typical American breakfast looked like.

Our cultural differences were many, but we shared a hunger and desire for God. The Holy Spirit worked through me, a weak and awkward vessel, just as he had worked through the early Church. At Pentecost, the language barrier was defeated through the power of the Spirit working through the disciples, and the message was able to meet the hearers exactly where they were. What an incredible miracle!

It is important to remember that the Holy Spirit is working in your life, with your many inabilities and insecurities, and is ready to assist you in speaking the message of salvation clearly to others. Many are lost and struggling with sin, and the Holy Spirit is ready to empower you to be a clarion of hope and truth. As Catholics, we are not called to be the judgment of God upon others; rather, we are invited to confidently share our witness of how God has changed our lives, touched our hearts, and initiated change within us. Don't be afraid to share what God has done in your life—after all, it may be exactly what those around you need to hear. Be at peace; you have a translator who can make even the most jumbled witness music to your hearer's ears. Remember that the Holy Spirit wants to burn away anything that is not of God with fiery love, so that you can be entirely his. When the prophet Isaiah encounters God in a very powerful way, the angel brings a burning coal to touch his unclean lips (Isaiah 6:6). The fiery love of God made him a powerful voice to those he was sent to teach. God wants to speak through you, and he gives you the Holy Spirit to empower you to become he gift he has made you.

QUESTIONS

How did the Holy Spirit move in the beginning of the Acts of the Apostles?

What Old Testament stories stand out to you in comparison to the work of the Holy Spirit?

How can the Holy Spirit give you favor in speaking to those in your life?

Fourth Meditation

"For these men are not drunk, as you suppose, since it is only the third hour of the day; but this is what was spoken by the prophet Joel: 'And in the last days it shall be, God declares, that I will pour out my Spirit upon all flesh, and your sons and your daughters shall prophesy, and your young men shall see visions, and your old men shall dream dreams; yes, and on my menservants and my maidservants in those days I will pour out my Spirit; and they shall prophesy."
— Acts 2:15-18

Catechetical Application

How can you encounter the Holy Spirit through this passage?

What does it say about who the Holy Spirit is, what he does, and the gifts he gives?

Here, we see Peter step with confidence into the leadership role he was called by Jesus to fulfill: "Blessed are you, Simon Bar-Jona! For flesh and blood has not revealed this to you, but my Father who is in heaven. And I tell you, you are Peter, and on this rock I will build my Church, and the gates of Hades shall not prevail against it. I will give you the keys of the kingdom of heaven, and whatever you bind on earth shall be bound in heaven, and whatever you loose on earth shall be loosed in heaven" (Matthew 16:17-19).

This passage from Acts references the prophesy of Joel, which is fulfilled with the decent of the Holy Spirit. With authority, Peter speaks as the interpretive voice concerning Scripture, specifically the fulfillment of prophecy, and no one argues with him. Think about this. It is accepted and understood that Peter is "getting the interpretation right," and those who hear him willingly fall in step with his role as leader of the Church. Peter is the definitive voice concerning a proper understanding of the Old Testament. It is worth noting that Acts 1:6 recounts how the disciples ask Jesus if the kingdom would be restored to Israel now that he is risen. But Jesus replies that it isn't for them to know specific times and seasons. What Jesus does tell them is that they shall receive power to witness (Acts 1:8). That is what Peter reminds the others when deciding who will take Judas' place; the person must be a witness of the resurrection (1:22). When Peter addresses the crowd, he stands with the Eleven (1:14) and speaks about the saving work of God to all dwelling in Jerusalem. This fulfills Jesus' instruction them to use their power to witness.

PRACTICAL APPLICATION

What does this passage say to you about your own life?

We are given power. This power is not granted so that we can rid ourselves of every obstacle or inconvenience nor to live comfortable lives, as if we have completed the race. The power we are given is the Spirit of God, and we receive him to testify to God's work in our lives. The impact of the Spirit in us can be seen by others and can cause wonder—and even misunderstanding. Those who witnessed the disciples filled with the Holy Spirit and speaking in tongues on Pentecost were amazed, and these witnesses incorrectly (and illogically) concluded that the disciples must have been drunk. Of course, this did not explain how everyone heard the Gospel in their own language.

Each of us has a way we communicate, both with our words and our actions. We tell a story by how we act and what we say. It is possible that the work God is doing in and through us is confusing to some and misunderstood by others, but our call is to witness the saving work of God to those around us. We are given power in the Holy Spirit to declare with our lives that God is still alive, and we are living proof that he still performs miracles.

How often do we waste time comparing ourselves to others? We may wish that we could look like another, be as smart or funny as someone else, or even be as "good" as another. When we compare ourselves to others we forget how unique and special we are—and the specific work God calls us to. Comparing ourselves with others can rob us of the opportunity to witness the work of God. Think of the passage from Acts: Some are prophetic, but others dream dreams; some have visions, but all who believe in Christ receive the Holy Spirit.

For those who heard this prophecy of Joel in Acts, seeing that it had just been fulfilled, it brought to mind so many other wonderful Old Testament prophecies: the dreams and visions of Joseph (Genesis 37), as well as those of Isaiah, Jeremiah, and Ezekiel—all promising Israel's restoration and salvation. Peter declares that the day has come in which the Spirit of God will come upon all flesh. You and I have received this same Spirit at baptism and confirmation, and we have the opportunity to be prophetic and a vision of hope amidst hopelessness by the way we live. These are, in fact, exciting times to be a part of, and knowing that the Holy Spirit is alive you should bring confidence.

QUESTIONS

When you compare yourself to others, what do you see in them that you don't see in yourself? Does this ever help you to live more fully for God?

What unique gifts and talents do you have to witness to God's work in your life to others?

How has God touched your life? How can you share this experience of God with others?

Fifth Meditation

*"Now when they heard this they were cut to the heart, and
said to Peter and the rest of the apostles, 'Brethren, what shall
we do?' And Peter said to them, 'Repent, and be baptized every
one of you in the name of Jesus Christ for the forgiveness
of your sins; and you shall receive the gift of the Holy Spirit.
For the promise is to you and to your children and to all that
are far off, every one whom the Lord our God calls to him.'
... 'And they held steadfastly to the apostles' teaching and
fellowship, to the breaking of the bread and to the prayers.'*
– Acts 2:37-39, 42

Catechetical Application

How can you encounter the Holy Spirit through this passage?

*What does it say about who the Holy Spirit is, what he does, and
the gifts he gives?*

These first few chapters of Acts pack quite a punch. There is
so much to reflect upon! After Peter speaks about the fulfillment
of Joel's prophecy, he preaches about the crucifixion of Jesus and
his victorious resurrection, as foretold by David. The response to
Peter's witness is a sincere desire among his hearers for conversion.
It really is a beautiful account, in which we are given a picture
of the very first converts to Christianity. It is interesting to note
that the assembled crowd, having heard of Jesus' death and

resurrection, want to know what to do. Peter tells them to repent and be baptized in the name of Jesus Christ for the forgiveness of sins. Then they too will receive the gift of the Holy Spirit.

Many things would have come to mind for a Jewish listener: the call to repentance, given by so many prophets of old; the work of John the Baptist, who not only preached repentance but also baptized those who repented. It is these early followers of John the Baptist who now see all that they learned from him fulfilled in Jesus. The message of Jesus' love for all, demonstrated upon the cross, will bring about the forgiveness needed by those who had come to Jerusalem to offer sacrifices for their sins. Peter tells them that true repentance is given through the sacrifice of Jesus. Sins are truly forgiven through the blood of Christ, not simply atoned for by the shedding of the blood of an animal. Not only are their sins forgiven, but they will receive the gift of the Holy Spirit. The result of this evangelical moment is the conversion of about three thousand people (Acts 2:41). We are then told in verse 42 that those who believed the message preached by the apostles held steadfastly to their teaching and fellowship, as well as to the breaking of the bread and prayers. How amazing it would have been to just sit and talk with the apostles about the life of Jesus!

PRACTICAL APPLICATION

What does this passage say to you about your own life?

Do you remember that moment in your life when you became a Christian? For most of us the answer is likely no; we became Christians when we were baptized as babies. Remember: In baptism, we become the recipients of the work of the Spirit spoken about in the Acts of the Apostles. Some of us may not have grown up in a faith-filled home and may have come to believe in Jesus later in life. What was it like to finally hear and believe the Gospel message for the first time? To realize that it was Jesus you were looking for all along—and to make the commitment to follow him. Everyone who comes to faith in Jesus has a story, even those who were baptized as infants or young children. We all had a moment where it all "clicked," and every day we have the opportunity to continue to say "yes" to God's work in our lives.

In many ways, the phrase "they held steadfastly" is meant to apply to each of us as we continue our journey towards eternity. We are called to continue holding steadfastly to the teachings of the Church and the gift of Jesus in the sacraments. The teachings and fellowship of the apostles continue to be given through the Church, and we are given the strength to hold steadfastly to Christ when we receive him in the Holy Eucharist, the greatest of all prayers. Jesus continually invites us into a relationship with him, a relationship based on the forgiveness of our sins. How does this happen? Through Christ's salvific death on the cross. How can we be a part of it? By receiving the forgiveness of sins through repentance and receiving his grace in the sacraments, particularly the Eucharist.

When my wife, Linda, and I graduated from high school, we decided to attend a college on the other side of the state, and we had to attend a student orientation. This was way before the days of GPS and smartphones, so we needed to rely on maps that showed many, but not all, of the roads to our destination. Based on our map calculations, we figured it would take us the entire night to drive from southwestern Florida to our college on the East Coast. We actually arrived at our destination in only three-and-a-half hours, and we ended up sleeping in our car. Disheveled and tired, cramped and uncomfortable, we went to wash up in the school's bathroom, only to discover that I had locked the keys in the car. Wondering what to do, a student from the school came over and helped us out. That student's kindness made me want to attend that college even more.

While living in southeastern Florida, I met John, a young biker who had had a rough life and looked like he had already lived a hundred years. John was radical for God. He was a bit in your face about his faith—and everything else, for that matter. I found that appealing. You never wondered how John felt about anything; he just told you, and he didn't seem to care if you agreed with him or not. One day John told me his story. He spent all his time and money in the biker scene, and he had customized his Harley Davidson to perfection. You could say that working on bikes was his god. Then, he began to wake up in the middle of the night in a cold sweat. Panicked, his heart raced with the reality of his existence and the realization of his mortality. He wondered, *Why am I here? Is there any meaning to life? Is there a God?* He began to read everything he could about Eastern spirituality, New Age ideas, and various religions, but nothing could answer his questions or bring him peace.

One day, John saw a paperback Bible in a thrift store and bought it. He said that he began reading on page one and kept reading the Bible every night trying to find answers. The more he read, the greater his conviction became. And the more he became afraid. He knew that he had broken every one of the Ten Commandments and that he had hated God's Chosen People. He was so ashamed that he used a razor blade to try and scrape off the swastika tattoo on his arm, yet he didn't find peace. He continued to plow through the rest of the Bible—and, as he says, "Somewhere in there I met Jesus." He had found Christ, or rather Christ found him. His repentance was total, and he gave up his old life entirely. John now wants nothing more than to tell people about the God who loves him and changed him. Though he still looks a little scary and rough around the edges, when you talk to him you see his joy and passion for Jesus. He knows Jesus, and you can be sure he is going to tell you about him.

QUESTIONS

Do you remember when you met Christ?

How easy is it for you to share your story of conversion?

How are you still participating in conversion?

What role does the Church have in your relationship with Jesus?

Sixth Meditation

"And Peter said to them, 'Repent, and be baptized every one of you in the name of Jesus Christ for the forgiveness of your sins; and you shall receive the gift of the Holy Spirit.'"

– Acts 2:38

Catechetical Application

How can you encounter the Holy Spirit through this passage?

What does this text say about who the Holy Spirit is, what he does, and the gifts he gives?

Repent! That word often ushers in visions of puritanical preachers, invoking hell-fire and brimstone with each provocative sentence. Repentance, though, is the very foundation of our Christian experience, and it is an essential part of the message of the apostles. Repentance is to turn away from sin and be truly sorry for doing what we should not or for not doing what we should. Think of the words we say in Mass: *I confess to Almighty God and to you my brothers and sisters that I have greatly sinned.* This Penitential Rite is vital, if we don't willingly confess our sins thinking we've not actually been sinful, St. John says we lie. The connection of the Holy Spirit with repentance and forgiveness spoken of at the very beginning of Acts is still active in the Church two thousand years later. It is still necessary for us to confess our sins, to repent and live out our baptismal promises. The prompting of the Spirit of God to repent and be forgiven is a gift to each of us, who are so often prone to make mistakes.

PRACTICAL APPLICATION

What does this passage say to you about your own life?

Recently, I had the opportunity to go to confession. I absolutely love this sacrament. Like many, I have been frustrated by some areas in my life that God has been making me aware of, and it was getting too easy to remain in a place of unrest. I knew the priest from previous events in the area, and his insights were outstanding and my penance was very applicable (which, as you probably know, is not always the case! While there is no guarantee that a priest will offer inspiring or helpful counsel, we know that it is in the person of Christ that the priest gives absolution). I made an act of contrition, and then heard the words of absolution:

> *God the Father of mercies, through the death and resurrection of your son, you have reconciled the world to yourself and sent the Holy Spirit among us for the forgiveness of sins. Through the ministry of the church, may God grant you pardon and peace. And I absolve you of your sins, in the name of the Father, and of the Son and of the Holy Spirit. Amen.*

I was struck by the phrase concerning the Holy Spirit. He was sent by our loving Father, through the salvific work of Christ, for the forgiveness of our sins. We can sometimes disconnect the role and work of the Holy Spirit from the sacramental life of the Church, but investment of the Trinity in our salvation is total.

Another insightful reminder from my priest is that Satan is our accuser. The feelings of constant inadequacy, failings, faults, inabilities, or insecurities can be overwhelming and persistent. He was kind enough to ask me whose voice it was that regularly accused me. I thought about it and decided it was myself. But where did I get those words and ideas from? The Enemy knows how to whisper the words of discouragement that will best sink into our mind and heart. In a strange way, I tend to believe the negative more easily about myself than the positive. Why? Probably because if I acknowledge the positive I am afraid that I am inching closer to pride, which while appealing, is highly toxic spiritually. In addition, it is easy to see my flaws, so after a while I falsely identify myself with my weakness rather than with the perspective of God. The Holy Spirit does not sit back accusing me; rather, he forgives my sins. In my sorrow for my sins, he is sent to comfort me! Remember: Jesus said that he was going to send an Advocate, the Comforter (John 15:26).

It can be difficult to see the Holy Spirit as Comforter when our spiritual habit may be self-deprecation. In many ways, we spend a lot of time as adults feeding the insecurities we picked up as children. We must allow the Holy Spirit to renew our minds, to give us hope, and to comfort us in our distress. We are not abandoned in our sins, nor are we forgotten. The Holy Spirit has been sent to us by the Father! I wonder if you would allow the Holy Spirit to comfort you today as you become aware of various flaws and struggles?

There will always be an accuser who is exaggerating, deceiving, lying and manipulating you into believing you can never find peace or comfort. Satan is the father of lies and he has come to steal, kill, and destroy. The Holy Spirit, sent from the Father, is the Spirit of Truth testifying about Jesus (see John 15:26). What is that truth and testimony? It is *not* that you are unacceptable and unfit for healing or love but the opposite! The Holy Spirit comforts us so that we do not become enslaved in the lie that we are unforgivable. We are comforted by the Holy Spirit intentionally by a loving Father, being reminded of a brother and friend who sacrificed all so that you could be at peace. This is the truth!

Last night, as I was soaking in the healing of the Holy Spirit's forgiving gift, I was encouraged to look at the weight I regularly carry. In Matthew 11:27-30, we are given a wonderful reminder that the burden and weight given by the Lord is easy and light. His yoke is given to lead us, and his leading brings us to a full acceptance in God. The invitation to come and rest is not for those who *deserve* this rest due to perfect living; rather, it is for those who are weak and weighed down by sin and suffering. Thank you Lord for your mercy and rest!

QUESTION

How do you see God's mercy expressed to you?

Seventh Meditation

"But Peter said, 'I have no silver and gold, but I give you what I have; in the name of Jesus Christ of Nazareth, rise and walk.'"
– Acts 3:6

Catechetical Application

How can you encounter the Holy Spirit through this passage?

What does it say about who the Holy Spirit is, what he does, and the gifts he gives?

Let's step back a minute and remember that the author of Acts is also the author of the Gospel of Luke. In many ways, the two make up a single story: the story of salvation. This salvation comes from the person and work of Jesus Christ, who forgives our sins. The same Spirit of God who works in and through Jesus is the very Spirit working in and through the Church's leaders. Recall the story of the lame man who was daily at the Gate called "Beautiful" begging for alms from all who entered the Temple (Acts 3:2). Peter and John are petitioned by this beggar, and Peter gives the memorable answer quoted above. The result of this miraculous act brings "wonder and amazement at what had happened to him" (Acts 3:10).

The placement of this story in Acts by Luke resonates with his placement of the story in his Gospel where Jesus heals the paralytic: "... and the power of the Lord was with him to heal"

(Luke 5:17). The response of the onlookers to the man who is lowered before Jesus through the tiles of the roof and healed is the same: "And amazement seized them all, and they glorified God and were filled with awe, saying, 'We have seen strange things today'" (Luke 5:26).

The power of God in the Gospel of Luke, demonstrated in this healing act of Jesus, is now seen in the early Church. Peter asks, "Men of Israel, why do you wonder at this, or why do you stare at us, as though by our own power or piety we had made him walk?" (Acts 3:12). He clearly tells all that the power is from God, the same God who worked through Abraham and Isaac and Jacob (Acts 3:13), who worked and was glorified in Jesus, whom they put to death. The message always comes back to the story of salvation. Peter says, "And his name, by faith in his name, has made this man strong whom you see and know; and the faith which is through Jesus has given the man this perfect health in the presence of you all" (Acts 3:16).

The faith of the paralytic's friends in Jesus motivated them to lower the man to be healed. Similarly, the belief the lame beggar had in the gift Peter willingly gives through the power of the Holy Spirit brings healing in Jesus' name. The result was amazement and wonder—but also the call to repentance for the forgiveness of sins (Acts. 3:19). God's power in the Holy Spirit is not simply given so that people can be freed from physical illness and paralysis. While this can happen, the ultimate power of God is given to forgive sins. This is what Jesus says in Luke's Gospel—he does the miraculous work of physical healing to show that he has the power to forgive sins (Luke 20-24). Peter tells those at the Temple, "God, having raised up his servant, sent him to you first, to bless you in turning every one of you from your wickedness" (Acts. 3:26). Power to heal, yes, but also to forgive. This power from God to forgive those who have sinned against us is given to you and me through the Spirit.

PRACTICAL APPLICATION

What does this passage say to you about your own life?

The story of the beggar is truly the story of our life. We are longing for things that help us make it through the day. We work to provide for our families, but when we find ourselves unable to do that on our own, we hope for a friend to assist us. The beggar needs money, and he relies on the kindness of others to place him at the gate to petition those going in to Temple. People going in and out of the Temple were sometimes motivated to notice the less fortunate, and so he asks Peter and John for help. Healing power flows from Peter, power given him by the Spirit, and this is what we should focus on.

Jesus' saving work upon the Cross is the gift that satisfies our greatest longings. The power of God is not limited to only healing our bodies, but also our souls through forgiving our sins. "But what God foretold by the mouth of all the prophets, that his Christ should suffer, he thus fulfilled. Repent therefore, and turn again, that your sins may be blotted out, that times of refreshing may come from the presence of the Lord" (Acts 3:18-20).

We are the beggar, the paralytic, the ones needing to repent. We regularly ask—and even pray—for various things, thinking that they will satisfy our greatest needs. The sacramental work of the Church gives us what we *really* need, and through this work, we receive the grace that helps us receive the refreshment that comes from the presence of the Lord (Acts 3:19). The sacrament of reconciliation forgives our sins, and the sacrament of the Holy Eucharist feeds our hearts with what we truly need.

The Holy Spirit is the power of God, given to us at baptism, bringing about the forgiveness of sins. The Holy Spirit is the power of God, given to each at the sacrament of reconciliation, which forgives our sins after baptism, bringing the healing we so desperately long for. When we are open to the work of the

Spirit in our life, we become more able to touch the lives of those within our reach, giving to them not a temporal solution, but the gift of God who fulfills their greatest longing. The power of God, given through the generous gift of the Holy Spirit, enables these early followers to be witnesses of the resurrection of Jesus Christ, ensuring the forgiveness of sins. You are a part of this work of God, having been filled with His Spirit, and you have the opportunity to witness to others what he has done in your life. Can you be open to the power of God in your life today?

QUESTIONS

Where do you need healing?

How has your faith in Jesus helped another towards a healing encounter with him?

What can you say about the healing power of God given at reconciliation?

EIGHTH MEDITATION

"Then Peter, filled with the Holy Spirit, said to them..."
$$- \text{Acts 4:8}$$

CATECHETICAL APPLICATION

How can you encounter the Holy Spirit through this passage?

What does it say about who the Holy Spirit is, what he does, and the gifts he gives?

The fourth chapter of Acts is packed with amazing stories of the early Church and its impact in evangelization. While Peter and John are speaking to the people who are amazed by the miracle of the healing of the lame beggar, some of the priests, the captain of the Temple, and some Sadducees were annoyed at the apostles' proclamation of the resurrection of the dead in Christ. The Sadducees did not believe in this, and so Peter and John were thrown into prison. The high priest and the other priests discuss how to deal with them, and they find themselves in a dilemma. They realize that keeping Peter and John incarcerated would not go over well with the people who rightly attributed this miracle to God. When questioned, Peter is filled with the Holy Spirit, who empowers him to be clear and bold in his words. Peter reminds those in attendance that it was their decision to kill Jesus Christ, in whose name the lame man was healed. "Now when they saw the boldness of Peter and

John, and perceived that they were uneducated, common men, they wondered; and they recognized that they had been with Jesus. But seeing the man that had been healed standing beside them, they had nothing to say in opposition" (Acts 4:13,14). The priests, though, insist that the disciples stop preaching about Jesus (Acts 4:17,18), but the disciples respond: "Whether it is right in the sight of God to listen to you rather than to God, you must judge; for we cannot but speak of what we have seen and heard" (Acts 4:20). What courage!

PRACTICAL APPLICATION

What does this passage say to you about your own life?

The Person and work of the Holy Spirit empower and embolden the early Christians to speak the message of salvation. Think about it: both Peter and John know that those who played a key part in crucifying Jesus are the same people who are now persecuting them: "Jesus Christ of Nazareth, whom you crucified, whom God raised from the dead, by him this man is standing before you well" (Acts 4:10). They are filled with the Spirit to speak the truth of who Jesus is and what he has done. With boldness, they do just that, and the result is an increase in the number of those who believe in the Gospel. Earlier in this chapter, it says that the believers were about five thousand, and we know that they continued to grow.

We should be encouraged because these early Christians knew that they had to be true to their call to witness Christ's resurrection and saving work, but they also knew they needed boldness. It would have been easy to be intimidated by the very people who crucified the Lord. They knew they had a call to go and preach the Gospel to all people, but they encountered strong opposition from their religious leaders. Like Jesus, they found that those who claimed to follow God were not interested in listening to his Son. Though the priests knew Peter and John were uneducated, common men, they couldn't deny the miracles they performed in the name of Jesus. They wanted to find a way to shut them up, but their efforts were in vain.

You and I should be encouraged to know that when we ask for the boldness to speak about what God has done in our life, we too will be filled with the power to witness to others. It is easy to be intimidated by people who seem more educated, wealthier, or more influential than us. But we can speak with confidence and authority about what God has done in us, because this work—this story—is unique to each of us. The Holy Spirit does not care about your lack of education when it comes to being living witnesses to the Good News! Your personal story of what God has done in your life is not only of value, but it is a part of how we grow as a Church. As you share your story, it can lead people to want to know more about Christ.

Think about those who saw the healed beggar and were converted. The healing God has done in delivering you from your sins, which paralyzed your spiritual life, is a testimony that others need to hear. What do you have to say about what Jesus has done in your life? You may be apprehensive about giving your testimony, but ask the Spirit to give you the strength. Don't worry if someone thinks it is silly that you rely upon Jesus for your sobriety, for example. Don't worry if someone finds your insistence on spiritual growth a declaration of a weak mind. There have always been people who close their hearts to God's love. It does no good to remain silent to appease the unhappiness of another. Each of us has a story to tell, because each of us has received the Holy Spirit—who invites us all to speak.

QUESTIONS

What is the Holy Spirit asking you to say about Jesus today?

Have you ever thought about what your testimony is concerning Jesus?

What is keeping you from sharing your faith? Have you prayed for courage?

Ninth Meditation

"But Peter said, 'Ananias, why has Satan filled your heart to lie to the Holy Spirit and to keep back part of the proceeds of the land?'"

– Acts 5:3

Catechetical Application

How can you encounter the Holy Spirit through this passage?

What does it say about who the Holy Spirit is, what he does, and the gifts he gives?

The story of Ananias is not a comfortable one. It does not leave us with warm feelings. And those who experienced this event firsthand felt ill at ease: "And great fear came upon the whole Church, and upon all who heard of these things" (Acts 5:11).

During this early period of the Church, there was much unity and solidarity. As Acts says, "Now the company of those who believed were of one heart and soul, and no one said that any of the things which he possessed was his own, but they had everything in common" (4:32). They shared what they had so none would be in need. "There was not any one needy among them, for as many as were possessors of lands or houses sold them, and brought the proceeds of what was sold and laid it at the apostles' feet; and distribution was made to each as any had need" (Acts 4:34, 35). What we have in the fifth chapter is a very sobering moment, where a couple decides to lie intentionally.

We can ask ourselves why someone would do such a thing, but why do any of us lie? Maybe Ananias wanted to keep up with appearances and look like he was as holy as everyone else. What we do know is that he sold a piece of property, "... and with his wife's knowledge he kept back some of the proceeds, and brought only a part and laid it at the apostles' feet" (Acts 5:2). Peter knew that Ananias was attempting to be deceptive about his gift, and he tells him that Satan has filled his heart to lie to the Holy Spirit. In his Gospel, Luke tells the story of the wealthy ruler, and the words of Jesus to him are clear: "Sell all that you have and distribute to the poor, and you will have treasure in heaven; and come, follow me" (Luke 18:22). Money can do strange things to people, and Luke emphasizes its influence in both his Gospel and the Acts of the Apostles.

Peter says to Ananias, "While it remained unsold, did it not remain your own? And after it was sold, was it not at your disposal? How is it that you have contrived this deed in your heart? You have not lied to men but to God" (Acts. 5:4). At that very moment, he fell down and died. After about three hours his wife, Sapphira, comes in and tries to deceive the apostles as well. Peter replies, "How is it that you have agreed together to tempt the Spirit of the Lord?" (Acts 5:9), and she too drops dead. Peter recognized immediately that Satan, the father of lies, had filled the hearts of Ananias and his wife. The impact of this event in the early Church proves that God is with the apostles, and that they are greater than any temptation of the devil.

PRACTICAL APPLICATION

What does this passage say to you about your own life?

In many ways, this is a difficult verse to apply to our lives because we likely don't spend much time trying to intentionally deceive the Holy Spirit. We must step back, though, and realize that there are lessons to be learned from this story. First, the generosity of the Lord does not mean that we should sell everything we have and live in some type of religious commune. The early Church, moved by the Spirit and a desire to help everyone have what they needed, implemented an opportunity for people to give as generously as they desired. There was no manipulation involved or pressure for all to rid themselves of property and homes. What we see is a giving heart by the Church's members.

The lying of Ananias and Sapphira was intentional, and their sin was discovered. They weren't deceiving just a group of people; rather, they were lying to the Holy Spirit. While we may not understand why this couple lied, Peter knew that Satan was at work, and the consequences for such sin were mortal. The gravity of sin is seen, and its impact upon the Church is a sobering reminder that our actions and intentions are important.

How often do we minimize the severity of a sin by somehow thinking it isn't that big of a deal? Every sin is an act that somehow lifts ourselves up into a position that is not our own. When we sin, we declare that we are the deciding factor on what we do or do not do. While we certainly have the freedom to sin or not, the consequences are not necessarily dealt out according to our wishes. There is much about this passage that is complex, but we can be sure that no one else lied about the donation they made for the work of God. I think the key phrases for us from this story come from Peter, who sees that Satan is at work, and that Ananias and his wife submitted to his temptation, resulting in their lie against the Holy Spirit.

What does this remind you of? Think back to the Garden of Eden. Adam and Eve are called to obey God's command, but they submit to the lie of the Serpent. The result of this original sin is mortality. The same God who administered justice to the early couple, is the very God working in the Church through his very Spirit. The severe consequences of sin are still present, and God is still at work asking for those following him to obey his voice rather than the temptation of the Serpent.

QUESTIONS

How do you deal with temptation in your life?

How can you be generous with your finances?

Tenth Meditation

"But at night an angel of the Lord opened the prison doors and brought them out and said, 'Go and stand in the temple and speak to the people all the words of this Life.' And when they heard this, they entered the temple at daybreak and taught."

– Acts 5:19

Catechetical Application

How can you encounter the Holy Spirit through this passage?

What does it say about who the Holy Spirit is, what he does, and the gifts he gives?

Most of us know what it is like to be enslaved to a certain sin. I am not saying that I know what your vice is, but I do know this: we all struggle with the world, the flesh and the devil. Somehow, our world has convinced many people that doing what we want, when we want, with whomever we want is how to live a full and enriched life. This is a lie. Doing whatever we want, when we want, with whomever we want enslaves us. We become less human when we give in to every desire and passionate inclination.

The apostles were imprisoned by the high priest and the Sadducees out of jealousy. The people were listening to them rather than the spiritual leadership of the Temple. To remedy the situation, the Jewish leaders had the followers of Jesus thrown into jail. The problem for the Sadducees is that God had other plans. Not only are the apostles set free, they are encouraged by the angel of the Lord to go and stand in the Temple and speak about Life in Christ.

There is nothing subtle about this moment. When the high priest and the council seek to address these troublemakers they have imprisoned, they discover that they are nowhere to be found—even though the gates are secure and guards are in place. Finding them in the Temple teaching the people, they are brought in again. The only rational person in the bunch is a Pharisee named Gamaliel, who cautions the others, saying, "Men of Israel, take care what you do with these men ... So in the present case I tell you, keep away from these men and let them alone; for if this plan or this undertaking is of men, it will fail; but if it is of God, you will not be able to overthrow them. You might even be found opposing God!" (Acts 5:35-39). They have the apostles beaten and charge them to no longer speak in Jesus' name. Earlier, when charged to remain silent, Peter answered, "We must obey God rather than men" (Acts 5:29).

What is important to realize is that the Holy Spirit, having filled these men, will not be hindered or repressed by the jealous efforts of those who are supposed to be spiritual leaders. The Spirit of God not only sends them a messenger to free them from captivity, but also empowers them to speak the truth of God's gift in Jesus Christ, counting themselves worthy of persecution: "Then they left the presence of the council, rejoicing that they were counted worthy to suffer dishonor for the name" (Acts 5:41). The Holy Spirit is the deliverer who empowers them to speak fearlessly about the love of Jesus as Lord and Savior, and this should encourage us to proclaim boldly God's work, regardless the efforts of others that might oppose us.

PRACTICAL APPLICATION

What does this passage say to you about your own life?

I have never been arrested and sent to jail, but I have visited a number of correctional facilities over the years. The process of going through security to enter a prison is complex. The correctional officers want to do everything possible to keep their inmates incarcerated, and there are many who would love to spring their friends and family from jail. They will do anything possible to slip through security any item needed to set their loved one free through security.

As a kid, I remember being fascinated with Alcatraz, "the Rock," the famous prison in San Francisco Bay that closed in the early 1960s. I even had the chance to visit the Rock once as a young child. I recall being locked in a cell with little to no light and experiencing what many who had been imprisoned there did. That trip to San Francisco was the best vacation as far as I was concerned, simply because of the visit to Alcatraz!

Recently, my wife and I took our kids down to an old prison in southeastern Ohio, which had closed decades ago. The prison was a major presence in our area for over a century, its castle-like walls looking as formidable now as they had in days of old. How could anyone escape from such a place? Interestingly, a lot of prisoners did. So security there wasn't that secure. As my wife and I walked with a few of our kids through this prison, it was amazing to hear the stories of its famous inmates. Just as I had experienced visiting Alcatraz as a kid, my own children were given a chance to walk into a cell and have the door slammed shut. I am praying this experience keeps them from a life of crime!

Being imprisoned is nothing to joke about. Unfortunately, there are many people who have committed horrific crimes who deserve such punishment. In the New Testament, we have some examples of imprisonment that are worth reflecting upon, and the story found in Acts 5 is one such moment. The fact that the apostles were delivered from prison with the doors still shut and the guards still on duty makes their deliverance miraculous. What was meant to detain and prevent the word of God from spreading was ineffective and useless against heavenly intervention.

Each of us is filled with the Spirit of God and are called to go and speak to those within our reach. Many of us have been "imprisoned" by the things that people have said to us over the years. Maybe we have been told that we aren't good enough to teach others about the faith, or that we are unworthy to speak about Christ since we are broken and sinful. The Enemy wants nothing more than to enslave and imprison you, because he knows you have been called to speak about the saving work of Christ and wants to keep you from doing this. If Satan can keep you imprisoned, he will. He is jealous of your love for God and of your willingness to continue to speak about God in the face of opposition. Unfortunately, we often listen to the lies of the Enemy. But, like the apostles in Acts, we must seek to obey God rather than men, and that means that we cannot remain silent. Each of us has an area of our life that can keep us imprisoned, but God will not leave us enslaved by our sins. In Christ, we have been given the power to be free, so we must freely and willingly share his message with others who so desperately need his truth and Life!

Think of the Old Testament examples of captivity, such as the Hebrews under the oppressive rule of the Egyptians and the Israelites' exile in Babylon, when people such as Daniel lived faithfully to God amidst great difficulty. These events show the irrepressible freedom of the Lord in the midst of trials and tribulations. The Gospels, too, have numerous stories of captivity, enslavement, and imprisonment, such as the Israel living under Roman occupation and the imprisonment of St.

Paul. When we look at the story of the Holy Spirit working in the Acts of the Apostles, the theme of freedom is not only evident in the deliverance from sin, but also when those in prison are set free by an angel so that the Gospel message could continue to spread across the land. If the Holy Spirit can deliver those locked and bound in a physical prison, can we not see the Spirit of God working in our lives to free us from enslavement to sinful behaviors? Our God is at work in our lives, and we are meant to *be* a message, not to simply speak one. Freedom from sin and enslavement is possible, because where the Spirit of the Lord is, there is freedom!

QUESTIONS

What is holding you back from living your faith?

What are you enslaved to?

How can you see the Spirit of God delivering you from captivity and empowering you to speak God's message of hope?

Eleventh Meditation

*"Therefore, brethren, pick out from among you
seven men of good repute, full of the Spirit and of
wisdom, whom we may appoint to this duty."*

— Acts 6:3

Catechetical Application

How can you encounter the Holy Spirit through this passage?

*What does it say about who the Holy Spirit is, what he does, and
the gifts he gives?*

This is the story of the selection of Stephen and the other
six whose role would be to serve. The apostles prayed and
laid their hands upon them (Acts 6:6), empowering them and
ordaining them as the first deacons. The work of the Church
was increasing, and to ensure that the preaching of God's
word continued, the need for aid in acts of service necessitated
action. The qualifications for such a seemingly menial job was
specific: men of good repute, full of the Spirit, full of wisdom,
and ultimately willing to serve. When Stephen is mentioned, it
says that he is a man "full of faith and of the Holy Spirit" (Acts
6:5). What does it look like to be full of faith? What does it look
like to be full of the Holy Spirit? Stephen was a man filled with
both, and his selection proves that the work of God in his life
was noticed by others. While most men are not called to be

deacons, all of us are called to be filled with faith and the Holy Spirit. You and I can grow in the theological virtue of faith, and we are certainly given and filled with the Spirit at baptism. The question, then, is who will we serve with such gifts?

PRACTICAL APPLICATION

What does this passage say to you about your own life?

Each of us is called to serve the Church in some way. It may be as a lector, an usher, a musician, or a Eucharistic minister. It may be to visit the sick, or help with the parish youth group, or volunteer for the parish fair. We are called to serve, and the Spirit of God within us enables each of us to do this in very real and practical ways.

When my wife was expecting our seventh child, the baby's due date was around the 150th anniversary of the doctrinal proclamation of Mary's Immaculate Conception. I had grown a lot in my understanding of the Blessed Mother and was determined to do St. Louis Marie De Montfort's thirty-day Marian consecration. Realizing that my son was to be born around this holy feast day, I decided to ask a deacon friend of mine and his wife to be his godparents. They had a great love for Mary, and what greater gift could I give my son then godparents who loved the Blessed Mother? Right up the road from my home is a house of the Marians of the Immaculate Conception order, and I decided to ask Father Don if he would baptize my son on the Immaculate Conception. We took our little baby, Jude, up the road to the Marians and had our son baptized on December 8th, 2004. My wife and I offered our son the fruit of our De Montfort Marian consecration. It was truly a holy and blessed day!

The deacon was a good friend of our family, and when my wife and I had our first miscarriage I asked if he would perform the funeral service for our little Felicity. She was unable to make it full term, but we loved her and wanted to honor her. The deacon came to the cemetery, where we laid our child to rest among the other premature babies who had been placed to rest there. The joy of Jude's baptism and the sorrow of Felicity's burial, both of which the deacon was present, gave me a picture of the heart of our Church.

While I have emphasized the call of each of us to serve those around us, it is the Church that ultimately serves us along our spiritual journey. Letting the Church serve us is sometimes difficult, but that is its mission. Through the sacraments, the Church comes to us in the areas and times of our life where we most need Jesus' presence. I saw this in the person of my friend, the deacon, who served my family at these two very profound moments.

I am confident that our deacon modeled some of St. Stephen's qualities to us on those occasions. He was certainly a man of faith, full of the Holy Spirit. While I spend a lot of time traveling around the country, it is humbling to have others in the Church touch my life in vulnerable times. I am truly grateful.

Can you think of some of the ways God serves you through his Church? It can sometimes be difficult to invite others into our broken and wounded areas, but the Spirit has a plan. As Acts says, "And Stephen, full of grace and power, did great wonders and signs among the people" (6:8). Stephen served, and the Spirit of God touched many through his service. Would you let the Holy Spirit minister to you through the Church? If so, I am confident that it is exactly what you need in your life. It certainly has been true for me and my family.

QUESTIONS

Would people be able to say you are filled with the Spirit?

How can you allow the Church to serve you? How has the Church served you already?

Is it easy to see the Holy Spirit working through the leadership of the Church?

TWELFTH MEDITATION

"But he, full of the Holy Spirit, gazed into heaven and saw the glory of God, and Jesus standing at the right hand of God."
— Acts 7:55

CATECHETICAL APPLICATION

How can you encounter the Holy Spirit through this passage?

What does it say about who the Holy Spirit is, what he does, and the gifts he gives?

St. Stephen doesn't appear to be afraid at all. He is falsely accused and was dragged out to be stoned to death, yet he does not seek to escape or threaten. Rather, he accepts his death and forgives those who are committing these unjust acts against him.

PRACTICAL APPLICATION

What does this passage say to you about your own life?

I am sitting in the sacristy of a parish church, where the priests vest for Mass. A little more than an hour remains until I am scheduled to give a talk to those gathered. I am tired but very much at peace. I am thinking about the fruits of the Holy Spirit that St. Paul speaks of in Galatians, particularly that of peace—something that I have not always experienced in my life. St. Stephen appears to be a man of great peace. I tend to think that if I worry about something, then somehow I will be able to make a difference in that particular issue. Oddly, this never seems to work. I find that after hours or days of fretting over a situation, it usually resolves itself and I didn't help this resolution by worrying. My lack of peace was ultimately a lack of trust.

I know that God has been asking me to trust him more. Of course, that it is easier to trust him when I can see how the plan is supposed to work, or when I protect myself with "back-up" scenarios. But God doesn't usually disclose his plan in advance, and he certainly isn't interested in my back-up strategies. He is calling me to trust him, and the Holy Spirit is brushing off my old habits much to my irritation.

What I am a little unnerved about is that I say that I trust in God, but I worry and stress over things I cannot control and obsess over things that I can. In both cases, I am not allowing God to have the driver's seat. Maybe this is why I walk in "occasional" peace and not "regular" peace. I am inclined to think that many of you can relate.

There have been times in my family's journey where we have decided upon a course of action that seems crazy to others or not very logical, yet there is peace attached to it that seems to place everything into its proper context. There have been other times when I was sure we should do something, such as buy a new car because our old one kept breaking down, but the peace just was not there. We could afford a new car, and it would give us a reliable vehicle, but within a few months it would turn out to be defective in an area that the warranty didn't cover. Peace–or a lack of it–is a sure sign of whether an action is correct or incorrect. Peace is a fruit of the Holy Spirit, so we are meant to walk in it.

Stephen was a man committed to the work of God. He probably thought he would do that work for many years, but he became the Church's first martyr. As he was being stoned, we wasn't resentful but peaceful. His peace was so obvious, so profound, that everyone noticed it: "And gazing at him, all who sat in the council saw that his face was the face of an angel" (Acts 6:15).

Think of Adam and Eve, who walked in peace with God. After they sinned, they lost this peace. Sin wrecks peace, and is the reason many often despair. Peace in times of unrest, in periods of sickness and death, even amidst poverty and rejection is truly heavenly, and heaven would have us live in peace, even though our world is without it. The Holy Spirit would have us walk in peace, even if our flesh wishes to wage war against it. Peace is not a lack of worry or regret; it is the fruit of trusting God, regardless of a doctor's diagnosis or the loss of a job. Peace is a state of being in which we trust in the goodness of God, regardless of our circumstances.

This is where the proverbial rubber meets the road. The love God has for us is so profound that we can remain peaceful even if everything goes against our desires. The plan of God is often different—but always better—than we can imagine, so trusting him will bring peace. Sometimes, things turn out the way we want and we can often speak about the work of God in those glorious moments, but he is also present in the times when things don't go according to our plan. In the end, you may feel uncomfortable bringing food to the hungry, but discomfort is not a lack of peace. Doing good, even if this is uncomfortable, is an action of peace because it is a tangible movement on our part to say with our actions that love can be expressed in many ways. We need peace in our lives, and we are at peace when we trust that the loving Spirit of God has been given to us and we know that we are never alone, both in good times and bad. St. Paul said he had learned to be content in all things, in times of wealth and times of impoverishment, because God was with him. This is the type of peace we are given in the Holy Spirit. This is the type of peace we see in Stephen as he faced death for his faith in Jesus.

QUESTIONS

How easy or difficult is it for you to trust God?

When do you find that you lose peace?

Can you find peace even when things don't go according to your plans?

THIRTEENTH MEDITATION

*"And Simon answered, 'Pray for me to the Lord, that
nothing of what you have said may come upon me.'"*
— Acts 8:24

CATECHETICAL APPLICATION

How can you encounter the Holy Spirit through this passage?

*What does it say about who the Holy Spirit is, what he does, and
the gifts he gives?*

The story of Simon the Magician is very interesting. Simon
was quite famous in Samaria, and many people there respected
and followed him. When Philip preached the Gospel in the
area, Simon believed and was baptized. He saw great signs and
miracles performed, and he was "amazed" (Acts 8:13). When
Peter and John heard that the people of Samaria were receiving
the Word of God, they made their way there to pray for them to
receive the Holy Spirit. "Now when Simon saw that the Spirit
was given through the laying on of the apostles' hands, he
offered them money, saying, "Give me also this power, that any
one on whom I lay my hands my receive the Holy Spirit" (Acts
8:18,19). This did not go over well. "But Peter said to him, 'Your
silver perish with you, because you thought you could obtain
the gift of God with money! You have neither part nor lot in this
matter, for your heart is not right before God. Repent therefore

of this wickedness of yours, and pray to the Lord that, if possible, the intent of your heart may be forgiven you. For I see that you are in the gall of bitterness and in the bond of iniquity" (Acts 8:20-24). Wow!

In the fifth chapter of Acts, we saw that the high priest and Sadducees were jealous of the apostles and throw them in jail. The people who belonged to the synagogue of freedmen and others instigated many to speak falsely about St. Stephen, causing him to be stoned to death. We also saw Simon the Magician was struggling with sin. Why? Because he was likely jealous at the way God was working through the apostles, and he determined to buy what could not be purchased. The sin is called out, and he cries out for forgiveness.

We may not have attempted to purchase the things of God, but we all have struggled with sin. I bet it is likely that we have been bitter and jealous of others. Sin often causes hurt and pain to others, whereas the gift of the Holy Spirit brings peace and forgiveness. While we may not be called out by the Church for our sins, the Holy Spirit calls each of us to repentance.

Practical Application

What does this passage say to you about your own life?

Everyone has sinned, in some manner, at some time. People who seem to have everything together are probably just better at appearances. We often build walls and wear masks because we don't want to be hurt. We want others to look up to us and see us as strong and confident in our faith. It is difficult to have a particular sin pointed out, but if we receive such correction in a spirit of humility, great growth can occur.

Think about a gifted coach, one entrusted with training a team to compete at the highest level of their sport. We can imagine him or her not only implementing a thought-out physical regimen but also an emotional and psychological one as well to train the athletes under their charge. The well-known saying mind over matter is often true in the journey towards athletic success, and an effective coach knows his or her players well enough to ensure such an outcome.

Simon the Magician, who was seriously mistaken in his understanding of God's ways, can teach us much about ourselves and our own sins. Simon cries out for mercy, which shows that he accepted the reality of his grave sin and desired healing. We sometimes spend too much time trying to justify our sins, instead of learning from them and wanting to change. If we fully believed that the Church and its teachings have been given to show us the right path, would it be easier to accept our sins and seek healing in the sacrament of reconciliation?

There can be a tendency among Christians to lift up a person as a role model to the point of almost "divinizing" him. When someone is seen as having their spiritual life completely together, we need to be careful not to resent—or be envious— their holiness and even wish for their demise. Remember—Paul condemned the unhealthy tendency to idolize certain leaders in the Church, noting that some were aligning themselves with their "spiritual heroes," such as himself, Apollos, Peter, etc. rather than Jesus.

Maybe you struggle with comparing yourself with others. Maybe this started as a desire to be better or as an appreciation for another's holiness, but in the end it has left you conflicted and uneasy. To become aware that we need to be on guard against envy is a sign of a maturing faith. If we want to be a true gift to others, we must always be open to letting the Holy Spirit make whatever refinements and changes in our lives that are needed for true sanctity.

When we have sinned, the remedy is confession. To acknowledge our sin and ask for healing is how we as Christ's followers protect ourselves against jealousy, envy, and bitterness. Confession is the way we get back on track to true spiritual health. We all have a long way to go on our journey; none of us have yet arrived. But the love God has for each of us is so profound that he will bring people into our lives who can help us see that we are not a lost cause.

You may have noticed that this magician's name was Simon, and in many ways I think the juxtaposition of this Simon the Magician with Simon Peter is intentional. The latter was chosen by Christ as the first bishop of Rome, the first pope, after he allowed the Lord to shine his love in the darkest places of his life. The former accepts the mercy of Christ and set on the right path towards healing. What will your story be like if you allow the love of God to correct and heal you?

QUESTIONS

What are areas in your life that need to be confessed for healing?

How can you protect against jealousy and bitterness?

What keeps you from confession?

Fourteenth Meditation

"And when they came up out of the water, the Spirit
of the Lord caught up Philip; and the eunuch saw
him no more, and went on his way rejoicing."

– Acts 8:39

Catechetical Application

How can you encounter the Holy Spirit through this passage?

What does it say about who the Holy Spirit is, what he does, and
the gifts he gives?

The Ethiopian eunuch was a minister of Candace, the queen of Ethiopia. He had charge of her treasures and was in Jerusalem to worship. The Scriptures say that on his return trip he began to read the prophet Isaiah, but he had difficulty understanding Isaiah's words. It is here that we see that the Spirit spoke to Philip saying, "Go up and join this chariot" (Acts 8:29). There is no arguing, only obedience. Philip runs to him and asks if he understands what he is reading, to which the Ethiopian replies, "How can I, unless someone guides me?" (vs. 31). In this moment, fostered and capitalized upon by the Spirit of God, Philip begins to share the gospel of Jesus Christ. Starting with that very passage, Philip teaches a man hungry to understand. The teaching is of such importance and so convicting that the eunuch says, "See, here is water! What is to

prevent my being baptized?" (Acts 8:37). We see the work of the
Spirit in Philip as he teaches this man, but we also know that the
opportunity was from the Spirit, as was the hunger within the
man's heart and his willingness to respond. The Spirit of God
was at work, for the story of salvation is always at the heart of
the early Church. We will see that it is the very thing that St.
Paul will focus upon: the cross of Christ.

Practical Application

What does this passage say to you about your own life?

The Spirit of God is always creating moments for you to
share with others the good news of Jesus. Whether it is a word
to someone at work explaining why you pray before lunch or the
questioning look as you show up with ashes on your forehead on
Ash Wednesday, you and I have many opportunities to allow the
Spirit of God to create moments for us to share the good news.

I love how Philip uses the very passage of Scripture that the
eunuch is struggling with to not only unfold insights concerning
that verse, but also as a springboard to dialogue about the whole
story of salvation. The Holy Spirit is working in the hearts of
those within your reach, within your Jerusalem. Are you willing
to capitalize upon these grace-filled opportunities? Some times
are better than others, so let the Spirit guide you along the way.
The result for the eunuch, after hearing Philip's answers to his
questions, was to be baptized.

Not long ago, I was giving a presentation in the St. Louis
area, and there were thousands of people present. I began to
speak about the importance of grace and sacraments in our lives
to keep the fire of faith burning. My message was that we need
to take our baptismal promises seriously. I had the thought, very
strong at the time, that there may be some unbaptized listeners

to my talk, and that maybe they would want to be baptized right then and there. Many priests were in attendance, so I asked if there was anyone there who hadn't been baptized but wanted to be. In front of thousands of people, a boy jumped up and came down. The place went crazy with joy! It was an epic moment, one that I was certain had nothing to do with me working a crowd and everything to do with the Lord calling to his own.

The Spirit of God works in and through us. Often, we just need to open our mouths. Sometimes people are really confused and just want to know and see that God is present for them in their difficulties. Jesus Christ is the answer that people are looking for, and the Spirit calls each of us to a deeper understanding of the purpose and meaning of our lives.

Another story that comes to mind in this regard happened early in my speaking ministry. I was asked to speak at a Salesian Catholic school in southwest Florida. As I was finishing my talk, I had the strong inspiration to encourage my listeners to go to confession. There were priests sitting up front, and I asked if they would be willing to hear the confessions of anyone in attendance. Suddenly, about two-thirds of the students got up and made their way to the priests. Everything stopped! The confessions went on for several hours. I remember seeing a priest confessing to another priest, and I felt the Spirit of God working in ways that went far beyond any message I had come to give. The school administrators ended up rescheduling the rest of the day. It was truly miraculous. It was such a blessing to see God speak through me at that moment, to see the Spirit of God convict the hearts of hundreds of teens.

You are called to go, speak, and explain. Like Philip, you can be led by the Spirit to share the message of salvation. Just spend a little time and listen to the Lord working in your life. If you are willing, he is certainly willing and enabling you to share with others the good news!

QUESTIONS

How have you felt the Spirit of God speaking through you?

Is there a time when you felt convicted to say something but were a bit afraid to do so? What did you do?

How can you share the story of God's love from the Scriptures? Are there favorite verses that mean a lot to you?

Fifteenth Meditation

"So Ananias departed and entered the house. And laying his hands on him he said, 'Brother Saul, the Lord Jesus who appeared to you on the road by which you came, has sent me that you may regain your sight and be filled with the Holy Spirit.'"

– Acts 9:17

Catechetical Application

How can you encounter the Holy Spirit through this passage?

What does it say about who the Holy Spirit is, what he does, and the gifts he gives?

The strength of God's transforming love is demonstrated in this powerful passage of Scripture. Can you imagine Ananias' concern when he was told he was going to lay hands of healing upon the one who had brought so much evil to the early Church? The time of darkness for Saul was a time of purgation and longing. The realization of all that he had done to hurt the Church paled to the point of blindness when compared to what Christ had done to bring the early Church into existence. Ananias enters the house, and there is the blind Paul.

We read nothing in this Scripture that would imply Ananias was hesitant to go, similar to Jonah's hesitation to go to Nineveh. We see only a willingness by this follower of Christ to do the work God had called him to. Ananias knows that Jesus has appeared to Saul, and he even calls him brother. The role of Ananias here is healer and friend. His hands, unbloodied, rest upon Saul, and the graces of God pour into this empty vessel.

From darkness to light, blindness to sight, Saul is able to see this man who called him brother. Ananias knows that Saul needs the Holy Spirit as well as sight, and his prayer is one of great expectation. He is obedient to the call of God, doing what he has been commanded. The Spirit of God fills Saul, and everything is made new.

We understand all that God will do through Saul, and his relationship with the Holy Spirit will be so close that much of the New Testament would be written by him. The familiarity of the Holy Spirit to Saul would become evident in the Scriptures, but this is the beginning and we are given a wonderful opportunity to see the fruit of obedience demonstrated through Ananias. There is a lot for us to apply to our own lives.

PRACTICAL APPLICATION

What does this passage say to you about your own life?

One thing to realize from this passage is that we will never know how much of an impact we will have upon others unless we willingly obey the call of God in our lives. He does not set us up for failure but for success; we must simply obey. Often, we may begin to move forward in our unique callings but question what God has asked. The example of Ananias is one for us to imitate. He not only obeys God in leaving his home to go to this opponent of the Church, but he faces Saul and sees him as Christ does; brother. We must remember that Jesus invites each of us to go to those who have been overlooked or feared and see them as Jesus does.

I have a friend who ministers to inner-city kids. At first glance it would be easy to see them as thugs or misguided youth prone to deviant behavior. The work that is being done with these young men and women is grounded upon obeying Jesus' command to go into all the world and preach the gospel. Some of these kids have certainly committed horrible crimes, but my friend sees each of them as his brother or sister. He identifies with them and willingly loves those who may not naturally engender feelings of affection.

This week another friend of mine is moving from the West to New York. He is like a big Teddy Bear, except that he is covered with tattoos. The story of conversion in his life is profound! While he is certainly not the man today that he was in his youth, people still judge him based upon his appearance. For the most part, he is used to it. It isn't as if he can just go and remove the tattoos. When you spend a few moments with him though, something very interesting happens; you don't notice the exterior markings very much. Soon, you just see Christ.

I think Ananias is an example of how all of us are called to see people as our friends—and even family—in the faith. Jesus Christ works in each of us in such a way that we are taken from darkness to light, and he then uses our willingness and obedience to be a part of someone else's journey from blindness to sight.

Maybe you can relate more to Saul than Ananias in this passage. Maybe you need healing and empowerment. The good news is that you are invited into a relationship with Jesus so that you can be free to witness your story of conversion to others. Like Saul, you may encounter people who are afraid or unwilling to see you as changed. But be encouraged—you have a family in the faith who will be there with you. Remember that conversion is not based upon our work, but rather our obedience to the work Jesus Christ chooses to do through us. The Holy

Spirit is ready to renew and heal not only you, but those you are called to visit.

As a final aside, did you notice that Ananias went to where Saul was? I think that is something for all of us to remember when it comes to sharing our faith. Often, I think we want the world to come to us because we have the answers that they long for, and while it is true that we do, our call by Christ is to go to the world. Where is God calling you to go today?

QUESTIONS

Who do you relate to more, Ananias or Saul?

How can you see a brother, when so often you are inclined to see an enemy?

Where is God calling you to go today?

Sixteenth Meditation

"And while Peter was pondering the vision, the Spirit said to him, "Behold, three men are looking for you. Rise and go down, and accompany them without hesitation; for I have sent them.""
— Acts 10:17-20

Catechetical Application

How can you encounter the Holy Spirit through this passage?

What does it say about who the Holy Spirit is, what he does, and the gifts he gives?

This is a famous passage of Scripture. There was a centurion named Cornelius who was very devout. He gave alms, prayed constantly, and feared God, along with his entire household. In a vision an angel of God told him to send men to Joppa to bring Simon back to him. The next day, they make their way to Simon, at the sixth hour Peter, waiting for some food to eat, falls into a trance and has the vision where he is told to eat what is considered unclean food. "Rise, Peter; kill and eat" (Acts 10:13). He responds that he hasn't eaten anything unclean in his life and doesn't intend to start now. Three times this happens, and each time he declines. It is then that our verses seventeen to twenty come into play. As Peter is reflecting upon the vision, the Spirit tells him three men are looking for him. Peter follows the men to Cornelius, and it is here that we see Peter's realization

that the Gentiles have been invited into communion with God—
that all are clean, acceptable in Christ.

There are many things in this passage that remind me
of events in salvation history. First, I think of Abraham and
Sarah, who take and offer a meal to three angels. It is the angels'
proclamation that the following year this elderly couple would
have a child, Isaac. The three men looking for Peter invite him
to go to a house, where an opportunity for the salvation of those
outside of the covenant becomes apparent.

Three times Peter says no to the invitation to rise, kill and
eat. I had to think the Lord chuckled a little at Peter, who was as
tenacious and obstinate as ever. He knew the voice was that of
the Lord, yet he still continues to argue. In many ways, it is truly
understandable for a Jew such as Peter to stand so adamantly
upon the conviction that eating certain foods was forbidden. But
God's plan of salvation is for all. We are all invited to be set free
from the enslavement of sin.

PRACTICAL APPLICATION

What does this passage say to you about your own life?

Every one of us have been invited into a relationship with
God through the salvific work of Jesus Christ. While we may not
think of it this way, you and I have been called into the family
of God because of this story found in Acts. The message here
was not an invitation for Jews to begin eating as much bacon
as humanly possible; rather, the point is that all are welcome at
the banquet of the Lord. We are truly blessed.

On a more practical level, you and I will likely not be
the recipient of visions initiated from God or delivered by an
angel, but he is leading us nonetheless. Each of us can not only
hear from the Lord in a personal way, but we can receive God's

blessings from those he sends into our lives. When Cornelius sees Peter, he bows down and starts to worship him. But Peter says, "Stand up; I too am a man." He tells his listeners what they all know. That it was previously unlawful for Jews to associate with men of other nations, but God had told him not to call anyone common or unclean. We see Peter preaching to the Gentiles, and the world is changed as a result.

Sometimes, I think we get stuck on labels and the easy judgments we are prone to make about others. God has invited us to see people as beautifully and wonderfully made, to see that there aren't any among us who are common or unclean. How often do we allow our prejudices and trivial irritations to keep us from sharing God's love? Christianity is grounded in love, and this means we have the chance to extend that love to all within our reach, regardless of color, creed, gender or any other stereotype. We are called to realize that the message God has given us to share with others is far more inclusive than previously imagined.

QUESTIONS

Who are the "gentiles" in your life? In other words, who can you share God's love with that may be a bit uncomfortable?

How many times do you argue with God's requests?

Is the Lord asking you to do something that you don't understand?

SEVENTEENTH MEDITATION

"While Peter was still saying this, the Holy Spirit fell on all who heard the word. And the believers from among the circumcised who came with Peter were amazed, because the gift of the Holy Spirit had been poured out even on the Gentiles. For they heard them speaking in tongues and extolling God. Then Peter declared, 'Can anyone forbid water for baptizing these people who have received the Holy Spirit just as we have?'"

– Acts 10:44-47

CATECHETICAL APPLICATION

How can you encounter the Holy Spirit through this passage?

What does it say about who the Holy Spirit is, what he does, and the gifts he gives?

There are typically three positions when it comes to this matter of speaking in tongues. First, some are convinced that speaking in tongues is applicable for today and is a valid sign of the work of the Spirit within an individual. Second, others are adamantly against recognizing this as a manifestation of a genuine work of God. Finally, still others have no opinion because they either don't know enough about it to speak with confidence or haven't even heard of such a thing. Wherever you are at concerning the gift of tongues, I love that the culmination of this moment in Scripture is not necessarily the utterance of speaking in tongues; rather, it is baptizing of those who otherwise would not have been.

Peter has a radical encounter with the Lord, who invites him to eat what was formerly unclean food. We know that God is showing Peter that his invitation to a new way of living is not only for the Jew but also for the Gentile. Any manifestation of the Spirit, if grounded in spiritual fertile soil, will lead people to encounter Christ in the sacraments. Anything that would take away someone from the sacramental life is certainly a warning sign.

In the Old Testament, it was the tower of Babel that initiated the multitude of languages, due to the consequences of pride. This divided people and caused them to scatter into varying lands with those they could understand. In this account in Acts, we see that this multitude of languages is unifying in the Spirit, bringing people closer to God and his will. Tongues in Sacred Scripture are certainly present, and for a variety of readers you can remember encountering this manifestation of the Spirit's gift in some form and fashion.

PRACTICAL APPLICATION

What does this passage say to you about your own life?

Let's address the matter of tongues a bit further, and please know I am finishing a book on the gifts of the Spirit so this is not the end of my final word on the topic. We have seen that the Holy Spirit is working in the lives of each one of us, and as we move towards our end, we have been given gifts both for individual growth and the good of the church. One of the gifts for the benefit and edification of others is speaking in tongues. Most people are fine with this, although I am not sure many have seen it demonstrated in any real-life situation. Unless you belong to a charismatic parish, it isn't often that one sees the gift of tongues implemented in liturgical surroundings.

One day I was sitting with a priest friend in a car. He was dropping me off at my house after an evening of ministry together. He was probably the most charismatic priest I knew, and regularly spoke in tongues. He wasn't afraid to belt it out if you know what I mean. So, alone and without any fear of judgment I asked him to unpack a little more this idea of a prayer language, having given to him my earlier experiences and questions. I told him that I'd had some moments of disappointments where I longed for this gift but didn't seem to receive it, and that when I did "try" and act upon the gift already given, it sounded like my old pastor's wife at the Assembly of God church. In fact, I can repeat her phrases verbatim even to this day. We heard it a lot in that Church. I told father that what I had decided was that God was so merciful and understanding that if I was basically just speaking gibberish like a small child occasionally does as they pretend to speak another language, that the worst I was doing was being childlike. There was nothing wrong about my attempt, and I wasn't intending anything but respect, even if it turned out to be me babbling like a ding dong. I felt like God may give an understanding smile to his child who seemed to fixate upon a gift that may not necessarily be meant for everyone. Father let me stay with this perspective, giving me a sense of peace about doing this prayerful act without feeling like I had figured the whole matter out. I have continued to reflect on this matter, and thankfully have come to some deeper insights into the beauty of a prayer language.

One last story about this. I am a bit of an introvert, and while that seems odd to many, it is the case nonetheless. I don't enjoy constantly being "on", nor do I like to have loud or even much visible expression when I worship. I am private when it comes to worship, because that is truly me in my most vulnerable position. Usually I don't raise my hands because I can't help feeling that everyone is watching me as we sing a song. I know that isn't the case but I don't have to worry about the distraction if I just stand quietly. It's just me. One day, I was slated to do a talk at a very charismatic Catholic parish when the leaders asked me to come in to be prayed over before going out. Suddenly, about twenty people began to pray, all in different tongues as they touched my shoulder and back. I was overwhelmed. It was almost chaos for me, and I was unnerved with all of the touching. I couldn't understand a thing, it was loud, and I certainly didn't leave that experience with peace. I kind of wished they would have just prayed over me in English, that would have probably helped more than the memory I have of that experience now. I will say this, I am the type of person who is going to want all that God has for me this side of eternity. Nonetheless, I am still very open and looking forward to what God has in store for me. I think this is a good attitude for us all to have. I am so thankful this isn't the end of my story with the Holy Spirit and the teaching about the gift of tongues as a prayer language.

QUESTIONS

Do you speak in tongues?

Should we all have a "prayer language"?

Do you feel comfortable talking about gifts of the Spirit?

Eighteenth Meditation

"'As I began to speak, the Holy Spirit fell on them just as on us at the beginning. And I remembered the word of the Lord, how he said, "John baptized with water, but you shall baptize with the Holy Spirit." If then God gave the same gift to them as he gave to us when we believed in the Lord Jesus Christ, who was I that I could withstand God?"' When they heard this they were silenced. And they glorified God, saying, 'Then to the Gentiles also God has granted repentance unto life.'"

– Acts 11:15-18

Catechetical Application

How can you encounter the Holy Spirit through this passage?

What does it say about who the Holy Spirit is, what he does, and the gifts he gives?

Peter finds himself being criticized in chapter 11. The apostles and those brethren in Judea had heard about Gentiles, and when Peter went to Jerusalem the circumcised party decided to question him about eating with uncircumcised men. Because Peter understood how big of an issue this was, he begins to explain to them the series of events that brought him to that moment of going into the house of those uncircumcised men. I love his statement: "Who was I that I could withstand God?" Beautiful! Peter remembered that Jesus himself said that they would baptize with the Holy Spirit and that the same gifts God had given to them were now being given to the Gentiles. I think Peter may have come close to learning his lesson about trying to argue with Jesus. When Peter speaks of the Spirit descending upon them just as it had for them at the beginning he is referring to Pentecost. The same Spirit descending in the same way upon the Gentiles is why Peter is so convinced!

PRACTICAL APPLICATION

What does this passage say to you about your own life?

You may not realize this but you have been filled with the Spirit of God at your baptism. The Spirit of God worked within you as you prepared for your first confession and the reception of your first Holy Communion. The Holy Spirit was with you in a powerful way at your confirmation. He is present in all the sacraments—in the anointing of the sick, the ordination of priests, deacons and bishops, and in each marriage if they wish to allow him to move within them. The Holy Spirit is given to you so that you can know love, God's love. The same Spirit that fell upon the apostles at Pentecost is the same Spirit that is within you now! The same Spirit that fell upon the Gentiles, convincing Peter that they were now a part of the opportunity of "repentance unto life" is the Spirit of God within you.

What does this say about your life? Look at all that God has done through the early followers of Jesus. That is your destiny. That missionary passion is your heritage, opportunity, and legacy. Why do we think that the Spirit of God only works in certain people? You must recognize that you are not a blip or accident in the grand scheme of God. He has intentionally chosen you, and your only hindrance to greatness is yourself. We must be people who believe that God calls us to something radical and beautiful. He wants to bring that about through you. Be encouraged, you are set up for success because the Spirit of God is within you as you go about your day.

You may not travel to the various destinations that you read about in the Acts of the Apostles by people like Paul, but you are called and empowered to speak the language of your time with a Spirit-led conviction. I wonder if you would take a step out and see that you have a calling in your life to share God's love. If you do, I am not saying you will have an easy path, because frankly, many of the early Church leaders died terribly brutal deaths. I am in fact saying that you will make a difference because it is God working in and through you with his Spirit, to share the love of Jesus Christ. Your weakness and limitations are exactly what Jesus specializes in, so don't limit what can happen with a little "yes." The more you step out in faith and believe that God wants to work in and through you, the more you will realize that your story is like others before you who have said yes. Today is a big day for you. I hope you can find a way to say yes to the Spirit of God.

QUESTIONS:

How can you step out in faith and believe that God will work in and through you?

If the same Spirit of God is in you that was in the apostles, what can you do?

What greater "yes" can you say to the Holy Spirit?

NINETEENTH MEDITATION

"While they were worshiping the Lord and fasting, the Holy Spirit said, 'Set apart for me Barnabas and Saul for the work to which I have called them.' Then after fasting and praying they laid their hands on them and sent them off."
— Acts 13:2,3

CATECHETICAL APPLICATION

How can you encounter the Holy Spirit through this passage?

What does it say about who the Holy Spirit is, what he does, and the gifts he gives?

We often compare ourselves with others, even though we know that this is a fruitless endeavor. Often, we may attempt to minimize the struggles and frustrations about what we are going through because we know others who have a more difficult lot in life. We may try to downplay our successes because we know that our friends have not had such success, but this attempt often reeks of false humility. Sometimes, we just need to realize that God works in different ways with different people. In Acts 13, the apostles are worshiping the Lord and fasting. The Holy Spirit speaks. The message is simple: The Spirit set apart Barnabus and Saul for the work he has called them to do.

In this passage, we see that the Holy Spirit *speaks*. That in and of itself is fascinating. It is also important to note that the certainty of what the Holy Spirit speaks is acted upon without any descent. Here, we have a clear word from God the Spirit that Barnabas and Saul are called to a specific work. The missionary work that Barnabas and Saul do is unique in the life of the early Church. If people were inclined to begrudge what the Spirit was doing in and through these missionaries, it would have been to no avail, because what we begin to realize is that outward opposition or conflict is not a deterrent to the work of the Spirit. One thing that could have hindered this effort was an unwillingness by Barnabas and Saul to obey the Spirit. We can imagine if they tried to flee the call of God by simply reflecting upon the book of Jonah, yet, thankfully we have not only a willing party for the task at hand, but we also see a sensitivity to the Spirit that certainly should be emulated. How can we be prepared not only to hear the call of the Spirit in our life but to willingly respond?

PRACTICAL APPLICATION

What does this say to you about your own life?

That you have been called by the Holy Spirit to a unique mission in the Kingdom of God is not in question; rather, whether you realize this is the case in point. The reason there is certainty about this call in the life of Barnabas and Saul is because of some important truths. First, they are in community with the Church. It is not a novel idea that Paul pitches to Barnabas; rather, it is a promoting of the Spirit within community that provides the certainty needed to endure the task at hand. Second, they are worshiping and fasting for a purpose. That purpose is to discern and know what road they must take next. Third, they again submitted to the Church at Antioch, receiving their blessing and anointing. Fourth, the confidence of the word from the Spirit, grounded in the Church in Antioch enables them to move with confidence, able to face the coming obstacles. This is exactly what we need to remember.

We must be people who remain in community with all our fellow parish members, not just with those with whom we get along. When we look at the thirteenth chapter of Acts we see that in the Church at Antioch there were prophets and teachers, people of high standing from various areas. Having the community surround us, using their unique gifts and talents, helps us to have stability and certainty concerning our calling.

We must be people who worship and fast for a purpose. We need to intentionally ask the Holy Spirit to speak to us in a manner that is clear enough for us to understand. Fasting is something we don't often value and seek out when it comes to spiritual development, but it is very much a part of the practices of the early Church.

We must place ourselves in the hands of our Church, asking for her blessings and anointing. We need this to face the difficulties that will be revealed in time. And, we must move forward by doing what the Spirit has spoken. Being a doer of the word and not only a hearer is imperative.

Recently, I began a ministry to married couples. It is something that I chose to do after much prayer and reflection. I submitted my ideas and desire to my local parish and aligned myself with my diocese. I know this is what the Lord is asking me to do, and having the support and confidence that my Church wants this too is an affirmation that I am not avoiding community but doing what I can to expand and build that community.

I wonder what the Spirit is saying to you?

QUESTIONS

Have you been feeling called to do something for God? What?

Have you spent a lot of time praying or even fasting about what God might want you to do? If no, would you be open to doing so?

What is the next step?

Twentieth Meditation

"But Saul, who is also called Paul, filled with the Holy Spirit,
looked intently at him and said, 'You son of the devil, you
enemy of all righteousness, full of all deceit and villainy,
will you not stop making crooked the straight paths of
the Lord? And now, behold, the hand of the Lord is upon
you, and you shall be blind and unable to see the sun for a
time.' Immediately mist and darkness fell upon him and
he went about seeking people to lead him by the hand."

– Acts 13:9-11

Catechetical Application

How can you encounter the Holy Spirit through this passage?

What does it say about who the Holy Spirit is, what he does, and
the gifts he gives?

Sometimes the Spirit of God seems to act in a way that
does not fit with our age of political correctness. Paul, filled
with the Holy Spirit, didn't just suddenly pick a random person
to verbally berate. Elymas was a magician who withstood Paul,
Barnabas, and John, also known as Mark (12:12), from coming
to Sergius Paulus, a man of intelligence who wanted to hear
the word of God. Elymas wanted to turn the proconsul Sergius
Paulus from the faith, and it is this that caused St. Paul to address

him so intensely. The Scripture says that Paul looked intently at him and then spoke to him. There was no speaking behind closed doors, and no interest in trying to gain favor with Elymas to ease him into a different line of thinking. There are times such as these where the work of the Enemy is so pronounced and clear that truth must be quick and clear in its delivery.

Paul knew that this man Sergius Paulus wanted to hear the word of God, but Elymas was intentionally hindering this and because of that, the reality of who St. Paul was dealing with was clear. He calls him a son of the devil, and an enemy of all righteousness. Full of deceit and villainy, he has tried to make God's straight paths crooked. The result is blindness. Filled with the Spirit, Paul not only disciplines, but he administers justice. For a while, he is blind, and he needs someone to lead him by the hand. While we may think that is so unfair, realize that Elymas was intending to blind, or keep in blindness others by preventing the light of the Gospel to be spoken. In addition, Paul has a bit of experience with blindness and I wonder if it is possible that we are left feeling hopeful for Elymas. The result of this confrontation is not only the discipline, but also possible hope of Elymas maybe coming towards a true conversion of his own, but the proconsul believed and was astonished at the teaching of the Lord.

Practical Application

What does this passage say to you about your own life?

There are going to be times in life when we will come up against people who seemingly go out of their way to hinder the Gospel. The reason this happens is something only God can truly know, but Jesus left us the example of what it will be like to be a light in a place of darkness. Not only did Jesus tell us we would have to take up our cross daily in following him, but

James says that we should count it as joy when we encounter various trials. Jesus says we are blessed if we are persecuted for righteousness' sake, and if you haven't heard this yet, all the apostles except John died horrible deaths as martyrs. The early Church is filled with people who stood up against great adversaries of the faith, and many gave their lives to stand for truth. Here are a few things to take away from this passage of Scripture.

First, Paul is filled with the Holy Spirit. This isn't him being vindictive or angry; rather, this is St. Paul recognizing the efforts of one given over to the devil attempting to hinder the proclamation of the word of God.

Second, there are times you need to speak the truth, even if it isn't what people want to hear. One who speaks out against abortion and euthanasia is not going to be embraced by our culture, which has become infatuated with selfishness at the expense of human life. It is sin that causes us to devalue life, and it is diabolical to pretend that this is a worthy and noble act. That is to place a bend in the straight line of God's love.

Third, Paul knew what it was like to be blind, and he knew what it was like to be opposed to God's will. Remember, Saul held the coats of those stoning St. Stephen. I wonder if Paul saw a little of himself in Elymas? The hand of the Lord was upon Elymas, and we can only hope that he began to realize the error of his ways.

Fourth, remember that the word of God being preached was the initial task Paul was undertaking, and after the distraction was adequately dealt with, he did what he was called to do.

There are always going to be times in your life when the Enemy tries to hinder your efforts at speaking the truth. You may not even see the foe, but the adversary is always at work. We battle spiritual adversaries as well as human ones, and what may be of help is to be like St. Paul and speak the truth about what we are encountering. If you feel that there is opposition to your efforts at sharing the faith, you should speak against it with the confidence of one filled with the Spirit of God. Don't be afraid to point out the lies. God will not only give you victory, but enable a way for you to live and share the faith to those you are called to reach.

Some may be quick to exaggerate the power of diabolical opposition to the Gospel, but there are many who worship at the altar of reason and totally discount the activity of the devil. We must realize that not only do we have physical battles and obstacles to face in our efforts of preaching the Gospel, but we also have conflict with an adversary we cannot see. Having the light of faith enabling us to see and speak with confidence is what we need. For this reason, you are invited to be filled with the Holy Spirit.

Questions

What is hindering your presentation of the Word of God?

How can you battle the Enemy?

Is it difficult or easy for you to recognize a spiritual adversary?

Twenty-First Meditation

"And the disciples were filled with joy and with the Holy Spirit."
– Acts 13:52

Catechetical Application

How can you encounter the Holy Spirit through this passage?

What does it say about who the Holy Spirit is, what he does, and the gifts he gives?

In the previous verses from Acts, we saw that the disciples had been encountering difficulties with the Jews, who had incited a devout woman of high standing and some of the leading men of the city to persecute Paul and Barnabas. These two missionaries were driven out of the district because of this persecution. It is amazing what can happen when we listen to the wrong voices in our life. Amidst all this tension and opposition, we find the disciples filled with joy and with the Holy Spirit. How beautiful!

Practical Application

What does this passage say to you about your own life?

One thing we can learn from this passage of Scripture is that it doesn't matter if you are a person of high standing, a leader of a city, or even a person who is traditionally devout.

If you listen to the wrong message, you will find yourself at odds with God's plan. The odds are not in your favor to succeed if that is the case. In verse 49, we read, "And the word of the Lord spread throughout all the region." The word of the Lord is juxtaposed with the word of the Jews, who knew that to get these proponents of Christ out of their city, they needed influential people on their side. Keep in mind, the Jews sought to stir up persecution against the disciples because they were jealous. In verses 44-45, we read, "The next Sabbath almost the whole city gathered together to hear the word of God. But when the Jews saw the multitudes, they were filled with jealousy, and contradicted what was spoken by Paul, and revived him." What voice are you listening to?

Being respected in your community does not necessarily mean that you are invincible to listening to the wrong word. In many ways, we can keep going back to the Garden motif, where the serpent posits a differing word than the one God had given to Adam and Eve. The serpent always wants to oppose God's work because he is filled with jealousy and pride. We saw in the previous meditation how the Enemy can consume a person such as Elymus, and now we see how even people of influence and devotion can be moved in the wrong direction when they listen to a word other than that of God. Paul is not afraid to give the difficult message, and in this case, he tells the Jews that while they were the first recipients of the word of God, since, "you thrust it from you, and judge yourselves unworthy of eternal life, behold, we turn to the Gentiles" (Acts 13:46). This did not go over well.

Sometimes our natural tendency to stick with what we are used to can get in the way of the new plan God is ready to unfold. These moments of being taken out of our comfort zone can seem abrupt, but God is willing to inconvenience us so that his love can be known. When you find yourself being stretched and challenged, ask yourself, is this because God wants to do something new in my life? Is this something I need to stand against for the sake of truth? Hindsight is 20/20, and it would be easy to wag our fingers at those in the book of Acts and wonder why they so willingly stand against the things of God. But we do this, too. When we talk about others or are jealous of them, we are falling for the word of the Enemy, who would have us lash out at others. When we fight against the teachings of the Church because they are difficult, we are listening to the wrong word.

In my new community, several parishes need to be consolidated. This is not easily done, for obvious reasons. People who have spent their entire lives as members of a parish, and they are now are being asked to leave it behind and travel several miles to a different parish every Sunday. I both understand and do not understand some of the adamant opposition to such consolidation. First, we do not have enough priests to cover six rural parishes or the finances to keep them open, so what purpose is there in continuing in debt for the dozen families that are complaining? Second, it isn't as if they are being asked to travel to a new land, county, or country for that matter (Canada is close). They need to drive into the same town as Walmart, which I am sure they frequent regularly because it is the only store for many basics. Third, the young priest who has been asked to pastor these parishes has offered lengthy explanations, as well as much advance notice to prepare for the consolidation. He has even visited parishioners' homes to build a relationship with them. Yet he is bombarded, maligned, and treated rudely, even though he has the approval of the bishop.

This is a clear example of a group of people listening to voices from others who are trying to incite opposition to one sent by God to bring healing. It is like a child who is told to come in and put on warmer clothes due to the dropping temperature. His friends say there is no need, but his parents insist he come in to be better prepared for what is upon them and to come. The voices a child listens to matter, and it matters to us as adults where we lend our ear. God wanted to expand the message of salvation to all, and this was opposed by people who were jealous, who were used to things being done one way for a long time. Whenever we stand against what God wants to accomplish, we are sure to lose.

I am not sure what is happening to you in your community, parish, or family, but I know that there will always be two voices you can choose to follow. Who will you listen to today?

Questions

How can you know God's voice?

What choices are you struggling with?

If the Holy Spirit brings the disciples joy even amidst opposition, do you have joy in your life? If not, why?

Twenty-Second Meditation

"In past generations he allowed all the nations to walk in their own ways; yet he did not leave himself without witness, for he did good and gave you from heaven rains and fruitful seasons, satisfying your hearts with food and gladness."

– Acts 14:17

Catechetical Application

How can you encounter the Holy Spirit through this passage?

What does it say about who the Holy Spirit is, what he does, and the gifts he gives?

This passage of Scripture may be one of my all-time favorites, not only from Acts but in all of the Bible. It may seem an odd one to hold near and dear to one's heart, but this chapter is well-known in the story of the early Church. Paul and Barnabas are in Lystra and Derbe, and a cripple from birth has faith enough to be healed. Paul sees this by looking intently at him, and so he says, "Stand upright on your feet" (Acts 14:10). He is healed, and the crowds determine that this miracle is the result of the gods coming down among them. They see Barnabas as Zeus and Paul as Hermes, and are ready to make sacrifices to them. Paul and Barnabas rip their clothes and insist that they are just men, and that it is God, who made the heavens and the earth, to whom all the glory belongs. They petition the crowd to turn from vain things to the living God.

It is this context that we reflect on Acts 14:17. In the previous two meditations, we have looked at misunderstanding and conflicts in presenting the Gospel. First, we saw Elymas, who hindered the message from the proconsul, and then we saw the Jews, who stirred up discord with influential devout women of high standing and leading men of the city to incite a persecution against the disciples. In both cases, this was an intentional opposition, brought about by jealousy. Here, though, we have people who are simply unprepared to see the connection of these miraculous acts with the God of Israel. They believe in higher beings and powers, but they are grounded in mythology. Paul wants them to know that the message of the living God is for them, because it was he who allowed all the nations to walk in their own ways for a time.

Here, we are reminded of 13:46, where Paul tells the Jews that they received the word of God first, but rejected it, so his preaching turned to the Gentiles. In Lystra and Derbe, Paul articulates how God provided for them and left a witness for them to believe. He tells them that God did good and gave them rain and fruitful seasons, and he satisfied their hearts with food and gladness. I love this! Here we find that God was working in their lives, bringing them joy and gladness, all the while preparing them for this moment of evangelization.

Sin is so profound in its impact that it is impossible to restore a right relationship with God simply by saying "sorry." We see this in the Garden of Eden. Adam and Eve disobeyed God's command and died, spiritually and (eventually) physically. Their offense cannot be fixed by a quick apology, as if that would suffice. What is needed is an eternal sacrifice and offering of recompense by Jesus, the God-man, who takes upon himself the punishment for their sin. All of salvation history (all the Old Testament leading up to Jesus) is a catechesis readying the people of God for this ultimate restoration. The Law was given to show humanity their need for a Savior. It disclosed the holiness of God, and it outlined the plan he has for us, his creation. In addition, the way God disclosed himself through covenants, prophets, and patriarchs prepared the world for healing. God chose Israel to be an "elder brother" to the surrounding nations, demonstrating obedience and a way of life that would be appealing to others. Unfortunately, Israel struggled greatly with sin, due to fallen human nature. The Prodigal Son, for example, loses himself in sin but repents and finds himself, returning to his father. He seeks only to be a slave but his loving father restores him as his son.

In this passage, we see Paul telling the Gentiles that it was God who was preparing them, satisfying and bringing to fruition their efforts, so that they could be restored to God. He didn't forget them as he established the covenants with Israel. Through it all, even amidst the failings of Israel to love, God provided for his creation. As a proponent of this good news, Paul comes on behalf of God, filled with the Holy Spirit, to the surrounding nations to speak to them about a new way of living. Paul barely restrains them from offering sacrifices to Barnabas and him. Immediately after this, we read: "But Jews came there from Antioch and Iconium; and having persuaded the people, they stoned Paul and dragged him out of the city, supposing that he was dead" (Acts 14:19). He wasn't dead, and God wasn't done speaking through him to the nations.

PRACTICAL APPLICATION

What does this passage say to you about your own life?

Keep this in mind: God is not surprised by where you are at in your understanding of him. He brings people into your life so that you can know him more. Often, we get distracted or worried about basic things concerning our life; finances, health, education, etc. We have often wondered if God cares about those things since he has so many more pressing concerns. This verse is a great consolation. God knows our needs, our longings, and our hopes. He does care about the little things.

Don't be discouraged, because in all things God is preparing you to trust him and know him more. He has a plan for you, and while it may seem like you are late to the game spiritually, God has had you in mind all along. Be encouraged. Even if you are verbally "stoned to death" by people who don't understand your love for others, realize you are in good company. If you are breathing, you have work to do.

Questions

How has God prepared your heart for him?

What makes you happy?

What obstacles are you facing?

TWENTY-THIRD MEDITATION

*"For it has seemed good to the Holy Spirit and to us to lay
upon you no greater burden than these necessary things: that
you abstain from what has been sacrificed to idols and from
blood and from what is strangled and from unchastity. If you
keep yourselves from these, you will do well. Farewell."*
— Acts 15:28,29

CATECHETICAL APPLICATION

How can you encounter the Holy Spirit through this passage?

*What does it say about who the Holy Spirit is, what he does, and
the gifts he gives?*

The fifteenth chapter of Acts describes the Council of
Jerusalem, and so it touches on the authority of the Church
in making decisions on faith and morality. What we see is
that certain people were insisting that everyone needed to be
circumcised according to the law of Moses to be saved, including
the Gentiles. While Paul and Barnabas argue against this
teaching, they go to Jerusalem to discuss this important issue
with the apostles and elders. Peter speaks about the importance
of the Gentiles being included in the receptivity of the Holy
Spirit, and James follows up by articulating what they have
decided. They insist that people abstain from food sacrificed
to idols, from unchastity, and from what is strangled and from

blood. That was it. So they write a letter and send Judas and Silas with a clear message for believers. I love the little phrase, "Since we have heard that some persons from us have troubled you with words, unsettling your minds, although we gave them no instructions" (Acts 15:24). So that there could be clarity in the matter, these messengers give them the message of what seemed good to the Holy Spirit and to "us" concerning this matter of circumcision. This message was received with great joy by those in Antioch.

PRACTICAL APPLICATION

What does this passage say to you about your own life?

If you want to know what the Holy Spirit is asking of you on matters of salvation, look to the Church. Why? Because it is the establishment that God has given so that we have a consistent teaching. You can see the Holy Spirit at work in very human men, yet the gift of God is something he foretold when Jesus said that the gates of hell would not prevail against the Church. The Spirit of God moves in the Church, with Peter its head and the elders gathered, and they deal decisively with a matter of salvation and moral integrity. Notice what the Church says matters more than an individual's interpretation. For Catholics, fidelity to Church authority is a work of the Spirit of God that enables us to trust with complete confidence. Many scoff at such allegiance, but trying to determine on one's own how to be saved is an act of arrogance.

If you find that yourself struggling with something you have heard or read, check that idea with the Church and its teachings. There are so many amazing insights that the Church has presented to us for two-thousand years, and we have a wonderful opportunity to read and live these insights whenever we wish.

For years, people were gobbling up the *Left Behind* books, thinking that these literary offerings were worthy avenues to explore on matters relating to the end times. While this series was a great success, it presented what is a novel idea in Christian theology, an idea believed by no one before the eighteenth century. But what does the Catholic Church teach about the end times? That is the question.

Similarly, author Dan Brown made waves with his books that seemingly exposed the historical corruption of the Church, and many believed his false assertions. Unfortunately, many assumed these were well-researched works that exposed the errors of the Church, but they were actually total fiction. Those who turn to pop culture and its take on the Church will always come up short when it comes to learning the truth about Catholicism. But how does the Church respond?

Most have read very little that is actually published by the Church. Not only has the Church spoken many times over the centuries about and against false teachings, she has guided the faithful in a deeper understanding of prayer, Mary, St. Joseph, faith and reason, and a host of other important matters of faith and morality. Why don't people read what the Church says? Because it is easier to believe stereotypes and misconceptions rather than the truth. Prejudice against the Catholic Faith may be one of the last acceptable areas of bigotry in our culture.

I encourage you to jump in and read what the Church says about who you are and what life is all about. I recommend starting with the *Catechism of the Catholic Church*. It is filled with amazing cross-references for those interested in going even deeper. The only problem with reading more about the Church from the Church's point of view is that you will realize just how much our culture gets wrong about our Faith.

QUESTIONS

Why do you believe what you do?

Have you ever read the Catechism of the Catholic Church?

When you struggle with an issues of faith, where do you turn for answers?

Twenty-Fourth Meditation

"And after some days Paul said to Barnabas, 'Come, let us return and visit the brethren in every city where we proclaimed the word of the Lord, and see how they are.' And Barnabas wanted to take with them John called Mark. But Paul thought best not to take with them one who had withdrawn from them in Pamphylia, and had not gone with them to the work. And there arose a sharp contention, so that they separated from each other; Barnabas took Mark with him and sailed away to Cyprus, but Paul chose Silas and departed, being commended by the brethren to the grace of the Lord. And he went through Syria and Cilicia, strengthening the churches."

– Acts 15:36-41

Catechetical Application

How can you encounter the Holy Spirit through this passage?

What does it say about who the Holy Spirit is, what he does, and the gifts he gives?

This is such a human moment for these men who have been called to evangelize the world. These leading proponents of the Good News engage in an argument, and it is so intense they split up and head their separate ways. These men, who have touched countless lives for the Kingdom of God, have a difference of opinion on how to proceed, and it is anything but peaceful.

We might imagine that all the early saints were completely indifferent to the struggles we face in our day and age, but here we see that they too had disagreements and imperfections.

Practical Application

What does this passage say to you about your own life?

Breathe a sigh of relief and realize that God is not through with you yet, as he was not through with these missionaries. There are going to be moments where we have struggles and difficulties working with others, even in matters that are of great importance such as evangelization.

Over the years, I realized that I have a somewhat unique style of speaking and ministering. On stage, I am very gregarious and fun, doing all I can to make people laugh and feel at ease, moving them towards a deeper and richer understanding of God's love. I spend hours talking with others, praying and answering questions, so that there can be clarity and healing. But I'm an introvert, so when I finish an event I feel like I have run a marathon—although I certainly don't look like I've ever run in one! I am drained and exhausted, and I have a tendency to avoid people so I can recover and get ready for the next event. I have some wonderful friends who are extroverts, and for many years I struggled with not wanting to let people down when I resort to my introverted ways. What I have come to realize is that I need to be true to who I am, even if many people don't understand me.

I think it is safe to say that these four holy men had different ways in approaching ministry because it was natural for them and what they felt God called them to. Paul wanted to go back and help those they worked with previously to grow in their faith. He wanted to check up on them, because he had a teacher's and a father's heart. Barnabas and Mark wanted to keep expanding the Church into new territories. Interestingly, God used all these men in different ways to accomplish what needed to be done.

You are not going to be like everyone else when it comes to serving God, and you will likely not get along perfectly with everyone you serve with. The best you can do is the best you can do. Rest in knowing that your lack of perfection is not a surprise to God—and that he is working with you where you are at, with who you are.

QUESTIONS

How easy is it for you to get along with others?

What makes you thrive? Being with many people or a few?

Have you disagreed with someone on something important? How do you deal with conflict?

Twenty-Fifth Meditation

*"And they went through the region of Phrygia
and Galatia, having been forbidden by the
Holy Spirit to speak the word in Asia."*

– Acts 16:6,7

Catechetical Application

How can you encounter the Holy Spirit through this passage?

*What does it say about who the Holy Spirit is, what he does, and
the gifts he gives?*

This is one of the few times in Scripture that the Holy
Spirit forbids someone to speak the Word of God in a given area.
In many ways, these verses are packed with more questions
than answers. Why did they choose to go through Phrygia and
Galatia after realizing they were not going through Asia? What
was their response when they heard the Holy Spirit say they
were forbidden to go to Asia? Did Silas hear this as well? Did
Timothy who was with them?

It seems almost impossible that there could be a reason
for someone not to go to a given area to preach the Gospel, but
we must remember that it was the Holy Spirit who was at work
in preparing hearts to hear this message. For some reason, this
was not the proper time for these men to preach the Good News
in that region.

PRACTICAL APPLICATION

What does this passage say to you about your own life?

While this may be simplistic, there are better times for us to speak about Christ to those within our reach than others. The Holy Spirit within you is going to nudge you when it is time to speak and encourage you to remain silent when that is the best course of action. What we begin to realize is that a relationship with the Holy Spirit is just that—a relationship. We need to spend time listening to the Spirit of God to know his voice.

Anyone who has been married for any length of time knows that there are good times to bring up certain subjects and bad times. How do we know this? From the many years of growing in our relationship with our spouse. The closer we are to our spouse, the more we know what will help them in a crisis, encourage them when they are down, or make them laugh when they seem stressed. The Holy Spirit is aware of where we are spiritually, as well as where each person is within our reach. Maybe today you intended to share your faith with a coworker, but the timing felt off. It may be that the Holy Spirit is inviting you to wait a little longer because he or she is not yet ready to hear the message. We can't allow fear to hold us back in sharing our faith, but listening to the Spirit of God is enhanced as we grow in our relationship with him.

Saying the right thing at the right time is an amazing gift! I am sure you can recall when people have said the right thing at the wrong time. The difference in timing is something that we may not fully understand, but the Holy Spirit does. What we see in the Scriptures is that there will be times when silence is golden, even in matters of evangelization. It calls the mind the quote attributed to St. Francis, "Preach the Gospel at all times, and when necessary use words." Sometimes silence is golden.

QUESTIONS

Have you ever felt inspired to hold your tongue, even though you wanted to share something with another? What made you remain silent? Did you ever come to understand why?

Have you ever said what you wanted to say and felt that it didn't matter?

Were you surprised to see that the Holy Spirit forbid Paul and Silas from going into Asia?

Twenty-Sixth Meditation

"One who heard us was a woman named Lydia, from the city of Thyatira, a seller of purple goods, who was a worshiper of God. The Lord opened her heart to listen to what was said by Paul. And when she was baptized, with her household, she begged us, saying, 'If you have judged me to be faithful to the Lord, come to my house and stay.' And she prevailed upon us."
— Acts 16:14,15

Catechetical Application

How can you encounter the Holy Spirit through this passage?

What does it say about who the Holy Spirit is, what he does, and the gifts he gives?

I love that the Scriptures speak of Lydia as a worshiper of God, and that the Lord opened her heart to listen to what was said. I think we can all attest to the fact that there is a difference in repeating back to another what was said and really listening. (If you are married, you will understand this quite well!) She worshiped God, was open to knowing him and listening to truth, and was willing to respond fully. Lydia is so convinced by what Paul says that she and her entire household were baptized. The result? She wanted to respond to the goodness of this moment by extending hospitality to Paul and the others.

Not only do we see the Gospel presented to the Gentiles but also witness Lydia and her entire household becoming Christians. This is the work of the Spirit!

Practical Application

What does this passage say to you about your own life?

Were you ever responsible for something or someone and failed in your responsibility? I am sure you have heard the phrase, "If you are going to do something, do it right the first time." If you do a pathetic job, you will likely spend more time trying to fix what will inevitably become a bigger problem. We may have learned this lesson when we were asked to mow the lawn as a teenager. Our minds wander, the day is hot, and if we can just finish the job, we can get about our business of hanging out with our friends. So we are distracted, and we end up cutting the grass unevenly and miss spots. When we do a job poorly, we need to spend a lot of time fixing our mistakes.

The consequences of a poor lawn mowing are small in the grand scheme of life. When we get older, though, certain choices have lasting consequences, some irrevocable. A friend of mine had so many problems during his first year of college due to drinking that he lost his scholarship and was kicked out of school. Often, the choice to drink and drive ends in death, and an innocent bystander frequently pays the price.

We are called to live life to the full, and so often our choices rob us of being great. There is a call upon our life through baptism, a call to greatness. Lydia has determined to do things right the first time. She listens and acts with a decided certainty. She is responsible for many, and weighs her acts as not only a person of faith, but as a calculated business decision. (Remember—we read that she is a seller of "purple goods.") She knows how to make decisions, and her decision to respond to Paul's message is the most important. She embodies what happens at baptism, when each of us becomes priest, prophet and king. She sacrifices in belief of the message. She tells her household, and they respond by being baptized. Lydia then extends the benefits of her "kingdom" to Paul, inviting him to stay in her house.

What does it mean that you become priest, prophet and king through baptism? Why does this matter? Let's consider again the story of Adam and Eve in the Garden of Eden. Adam is placed in this bountiful garden, given responsibilities and opportunities befitting his role as one having dominion. We could say that Adam is a kingly figure in this kingdom of plenty. He is given tasks and warnings from God about what must be done and what must be avoided. When Eve is given to Adam as his helpmate and gift, it is the responsibility of Adam to disclose what the boundaries are, because this is necessary to keep order in the garden. Not only is Eve a gift to Adam, but Adam is to be gift to Eve. He is to disclose to Eve the will of God, and in many ways, he is to be a prophetic figure, obediently disclosing to those within his reach the will of God. This willingness to become gift to Eve should be fruitful. In addition, Adam is to keep the land, making sacrifices to ensure its protection and care. In other words, he is to acts as a priest, ensuring that there can be life and harmony.

The moment the Serpent arrives in the Garden, though, we realize something bad is about to occur. The harmony is about to be disrupted. Many ask why God would place the Serpent in the garden? Why did he allow such a terrible temptation? Remember, though, that God gave the authority, and responsibility to Adam to "be fruitful and multiply, and fill the earth and subdue it; and have dominion over the fish of the sea and over the birds of the air and over every living thing that moves upon the earth" (Genesis 1:28). In Genesis 2:15, he is to till and keep the garden. So how did the Serpent get in? Adam wasn't careful enough to keep the garden and protect its boundaries! He failed in his role as king; he allowed the Enemy into realm he was called to protect.

Adam also failed in his responsibility as a prophet, because Eve wrongly articulates God's rule for the tree of the knowledge of good and evil. God said that on the day they eat of it they would die, but Eve responds to the Serpent that, "You shall not eat of the fruit of the tree that is in the middle of the garden, nor shall you touch it, or you shall die" (Genesis 3:3). It seems possible that the addition of "touching" the fruit may have come from Adam. The problem isn't Eve's careless recitation of God's law; rather, it is that Adam is standing with Eve during her dialogue with the Serpent, and he does nothing to correct her or defend what he has been given! When she eats of the forbidden fruit, it says in verse six: "And she also gave some to her husband, who was with her, and he ate." So he fails in an epic way as a priest. Adam does not sacrifice for his bride so that she will be protected from death; rather, he stands quietly by as Eve succumbs to the temptation of the Serpent.

Jesus, as the Last Adam, counters the failings of the first Adam and invites us into a new way of living. He takes what God has given him, and not only does he tend and keep the responsibilities given him by the Father, he also fights the Serpent. The blood that pours down Jesus' brow at the Garden of Gethsemane is the sacrificial agony of a priest willing the good for his bride, who has listened to the tempting hiss of the Serpent. Jesus speaks the words of God to the lying Serpent as a prophetic voice in opposition to his temptations.

Jesus lays down his life as a priest, sacrificing himself so that communion with God could be gained through his obedience. He is the King of Kings, and his reign banishes the Enemy from his kingdom, establishing true dominion. Having been baptized and filled with the Holy Spirit, we are now invited to heed the original call of humanity to be priest, prophet, and king in Christ. We must willingly make sacrifices, speak and adhere to the word of God as a true prophet, and rule with determination so that the lying Serpent does not breach the area which we have been given responsibility over. Each time we sin, it is not because we are unable to defend ourselves; rather, it is because we choose not to live the gifts we have been given at baptism. The Holy Spirit is ready to fill us with a kingly confidence, a fearless prophetic courage in proclaiming and adhering to God's word, and a priestly attitude of sacrifice, because this is what it means to be born again as God's children.

We must remember that the Holy Spirit is placed in us so that we live this life in the most authentic way possible. "Christ, high priest and unique mediator, has made of the Church "a kingdom, priests for his God and Father." The whole community of believers is priestly. We exercise our baptismal priesthood through our participation, each according to our vocation, in Christ's mission as priest, prophet, and king. Through the sacraments of baptism and confirmation the faithful are "consecrated to be ... a holy priesthood" (CCC 1546).

A final consideration: Adam and Eve were called to be fruitful and multiply. Interestingly, their troubles could have been avoided if they would have simply obeyed God's word. Let us pray that we will be focused on living out our baptismal gifts and calling, avoiding the lies of the Serpent through the power of the Holy Spirit. Let us be more like Lydia, who listened, spoke, and responded to God's call, and extended gratitude. The more we do this, the more we will have spiritual fruitfulness, which will make us even more diligent in our commitment to God's will.

QUESTIONS

What does it mean to be a priest, prophet, and king?

How has the Enemy attempted to deceive and tempt you away from obedience to God?

How did Adam fail in his responsibility to tend and keep what God gave him?

Twenty-Seventh Meditation

*"As we were going to the place of prayer, we were
met by a slave girl who had a spirit of divination and
brought her owners much gain by soothsaying."*

– Acts 16:16

Catechetical Application

How can you encounter the Holy Spirit through this passage?

*What does it say about who the Holy Spirit is, what he does, and
the gifts he gives?*

We move from an analysis of Lydia, a woman who is
sensitive to the Spirit of God, to a slave girl who is influenced
by a different spirit. This girl is used by her owners to bring
them gain through her ability at divination. As St. Paul and
Silas were going to the place of prayer, they met this girl, who
followed them crying out: "These men are servants of the most
high God, who proclaim to you the way of salvation." She did
this for many days! After this, Scripture says, "But Paul was
annoyed, and turned and said to the spirit, 'I charge you in the
name of Jesus Christ to come out of her.'"

Here are a few things to notice. First, Paul is annoyed.
Again, a very human emotion, even in the midst of such
important work as evangelizing the world and spending time
in prayer! Second, Paul addresses the unclean spirit, not the

slave girl. He knows who is speaking. Third, the authority Paul has is demonstrated in his charging the spirit to leave her. We see that the evil spirit is obedient to Paul. The Spirit within Paul is greater than the spirit within this slave girl. This casting out of an evil spirit is reminiscent of the work of Jesus in the Gospels. Just as God the Father worked through the Son, now God the Spirit is empowering the early Church to confront not only physical but spiritual enslavement as well.

The result of this act is a very angry group of owners who realize their financial gain was now gone with this girl being restored to her right mind. They turn the crowd against Paul and Silas, publicly mocking them, tearing off their clothes and giving orders to beat them with rods: "And when they had inflicted many blows upon them, they threw them into prison, charging the jailer to keep them safely" (Acts 16:24).

You would think that this would cause Paul and Silas to be quiet, but no. The Bible says, "But about midnight Paul and Silas were praying and singing hymns to God, and the prisoners were listening to them, and suddenly there was a great earthquake, so that the foundations of the prison were shaken; and immediately all the doors were opened and every one's chains were unfastened" (Acts 16: 25,26). Now, that is amazing!

The imprisonment of Paul and Silas is just another opportunity for them to minister to those in captivity, and to show that God is greater than any physical enslavement. The deliverance of the slave girl from her spiritual captivity and now the deliverance of those imprisoned physically in jail is not a coincidence. God is greater than any chain, lock, or seemingly hopeless obstacle. In the aftermath of the earthquake, the jailer awakens and sees that Paul and Silas are gone and decides to kill himself. After all, he was specifically told to "keep them safely" (Acts 16:23). Now, all is seemingly lost. It is at this moment that Paul loudly says, "Do not harm yourself, for we are all here." How hard was it for Paul to keep the other prisoners there?

What was it about Paul and Silas that made the prisoners feel more liberated with them than if they had immediately run out without shackles? The result of this is that the jailer asks, "What must I do to be saved?" How ironic. The ones who are imprisoned are answering the question of salvation. "Believe in the Lord Jesus, and you will be saved, you and your household" (Acts 16:32). Amazing!

Not only does the jailer end up converting, along with his household, but we are told: "Then he brought them up into his house, and set food before them; and he rejoiced with all his household that he had believed in God" (Acts 16:34). When the magistrates found out what had happened, they went to the jailer to have the convicts sent out. The problem was that they were Roman citizens and had been beaten publicly without having been officially condemned. When the magistrates found out that Paul and Silas were Roman citizens, they apologized to them! After all of this, we find Paul and Silas visiting Lydia again. Can you imagine this time of fellowship?

PRACTICAL APPLICATION

What does this passage say to you about your own life?

This sixteenth chapter of Acts is so filled with amazing stories that I believe you could find countless ways to apply these truths to your own life. God knows your circumstances and times of being falsely accused and enslaved. While the Enemy may try to profit off of our captivity, God can deliver us physically and spiritually. While we may be spiritually beaten and even imprisoned, we must always remember that we are citizens of God's kingdom! In many ways, the people of God will be treated unfairly by the world, but it is how we approach these moments that not only impact and influence us but can also be a catalyst for conversion to others. The rejoicing and singing by

Paul and Silas impact the prisoners so much that they stay with them even with their shackles loosened. The willingness to stay and preach to the jailer causes not only his conversion but the conversion of his entire household.

Can you rejoice today, even though you may feel enslaved? Pray for an attitude that makes other people feel freer in your presence, that they may embrace the true freedom offered in Christ rather than what the world often promotes as "freedom."

Questions

Do you feel you have been misunderstood and even enslaved emotionally or physically? Where is Jesus in all of this?

Who can you witness joy to today?

Who is the jailer in your life?

Twenty-Eighth Meditation

"Now while Paul was waiting for them at Athens, his spirit was provoked within him as he saw that the city was full of idols."
– Acts 17:16

Catechetical Application

How can you encounter the Holy Spirit through this passage?

What does it say about who the Holy Spirit is, what he does, and the gifts he gives?

Here, we see one of the most famous moments in Paul's missionary journeys. It is likely you have heard this story before. Paul is in Athens, and he sees many idols, as well as the Athenians' efforts to understand deep philosophical matters. "So Paul, standing in the middle of the Areopagus, said: 'Men of Athens, I perceive that in every way you are very religious. For as I passed along, and observed the objects of your worship, I found also an altar with this inscription, *To an unknown god.* What therefore you worship as unknown, this I proclaim to you. The God who made the world and everything in it, being Lord of heaven and earth, does not live in shrines made by man, nor is he served by human hands, as though he needed anything, since he himself gives to all men life and breath and everything'" (Acts 17:22-25).

This gives us a picture of Paul's preaching style. He places his message in the context of the Athenians' inclination towards spiritual things, and he shows how much greater his God is in comparison. He tells the story of his God, who is their God too if they wish to believe. Two converts were Dionysius the Areopagite and a woman named Damaris. The springboard for discussion was that Paul recognized that they were religious people, and he used their own statue to begin a discussion on faith. He is aware of the beliefs held by the philosophers, yet he decides to speak about the resurrection of the dead, which some would mock (Acts 17:31). Paul is grieved, not because they are horrible, but because he knows that it is time for them to see what even their own prophets have spoken about—the one true God, who calls all to repentance and conversion.

PRACTICAL APPLICATION

What does this passage say to you about your own life?

Many things can grieve us. If we are not careful, we can easily come across as judgmental. Loving people who are different from us is not always going to be received with open arms. In all things, though, we must be people of great charity. Paul shows us that knowing who you are speaking to and what they believe is key. Why do people act and speak as they do? What is it that they believe, and why? Paul understood not only the Athenians and their propensity for idols and mythology, but he recognized their great interest in philosophy. Paul spoke in a way that the Athenians would appreciate, but he didn't shy away from the truths of his faith. Paul loves them, he knows what they believe religiously, philosophically, and even poetically, and that is why he is so effective in sharing the Gospel.

This reminds me of something the Trappist monk Thomas Merton said when first speaking of ecumenical endeavors, and then inter-religious dialogue. "The more I am able to affirm others, to say 'yes' to them in myself, by discovering them in myself and myself in them, the more real I am. I am fully real if my own heart says yes to everyone. I will be a better Catholic, not if I can refute every shade of Protestantism, but if I can affirm the truth in it and still go further." He then says, "So, too, with the Muslims, the Hindus, the Buddhists, etc. This does not mean syncretism, indifferentism, the vapid and careless friendliness that accepts everything by thinking of nothing. There is much that one cannot affirm and accept, but first one must say 'yes' where one really can. If I affirm myself as a Catholic merely by denying all that is Muslim, Jewish, Protestant, Hindu, Buddhist, etc., in the end I will find that there is not much left for me to affirm as a Catholic: and no breath of the Spirit with which to affirm it."

QUESTIONS

What do your friends believe that grieves you?

Do you struggle to share your faith?

Twenty-Ninth Meditation

"And he found a Jew named Aquila, a native of Pontus, lately come from Italy with his wife Priscilla, because Claudius had commanded all the Jews to leave Rome. And he went to see them; and because he was of the same trade he stayed with them, and they worked, for by trade they were tentmakers. And he argued in the synagogue every sabbath, and persuaded Jews and Greeks."
– Acts 18:1-4

Catechetical Application

How can you encounter the Holy Spirit through this passage?

What does it say about who the Holy Spirit is, what he does, and the gifts he gives?

Sometimes, I think we forget that Paul, with all his missionary passion and zeal, his sensitivity to the Spirit as he writes letters that will become much of the New Testament, was a tentmaker! He made tents for a living. With this simple and telling phrase, the average layperson can breathe a sigh of relief. You and I can make a great difference for the kingdom of God, right where we are.

Here, Paul leaves Athens and arrives in Corinth. We know that Paul has a great love for the Corinthians, and he will later write some very pointed letters to the Church there. He is now going to see some recently displaced Jews who had to leave

Rome. He goes to them and stays with them because they are all tentmakers. What a great business partner!

I love that Aquila and his wife Priscilla are mentioned. Think of the fellowship they had, not only working together throughout the week, but watching Paul, their friend, speaking with such boldness each Sabbath. We have work and friendship, and I think this is the foundation that keeps our head on straight when it comes to ministry. While Paul's letters are extremely bold and motivating, face-to-face he was unassuming and quite normal. What a relief. Paul clearly had an affection for the people he worked with and ministered to.

You and I have the chance through our relationships to be loved and share that love. This attention to friendship and work is important for Paul and for all of us. Paul tells the Thessalonians that if they will not work they should not eat (2 Thessalonians 3:10). This is not a criticism of those who are down and out, unable or hindered through societal or social constraints; rather, it is a call to recognize that work is a part of not only the human condition but also important in ministry.

PRACTICAL APPLICATION

What does this passage say to you about your own life?

When we were young and hoped to get married sooner rather than later, Linda and I surrounded ourselves with wonderful couples who modeled marriage and family to us. It was excellent to see the unique ways family worked, and we made great friendships that have lasted for years. The people we work with and surround ourselves with are very important to our ministry. Who motivates you to be excellent?

St. Paul chose to stay with a family. He worked with and fellowshipped with people, even within the very sinful city of Corinth. Having a community is imperative, especially when you are working. You and I can be encouraged that one of the greatest of all saints was a tentmaker and saw the value of the friendship of a married couple. Think about how St. Paul will speak to those in Ephesus about marriage, and remember that Paul stayed with holy couples who lived and served one another with excellence. You may be the family that encourages someone to become a great evangelist. Love greatly, work with excellence, and let that be the wellspring from which you gather the strength to share God's love to a world so in need of his mercy.

QUESTIONS

How can you strengthen your relationships at home and at work?

What type of community do you have at work?

How can you share your faith at work?

THIRTIETH MEDITATION

"He had been instructed in the way of the Lord; and being fervent in spirit, he spoke and taught accurately the things concerning Jesus, though he knew only the baptism of John."
– Acts 18:25

CATECHETICAL APPLICATION

How can you encounter the Holy Spirit through this passage?

What does it say about who the Holy Spirit is, what he does, and the gifts he gives?

There was a Jew named Apollos, who came to Ephesus, "an eloquent man, well versed in the Scriptures" (Acts 18:24). What fascinates me about this passage is that as he began speaking boldly in the synagogue, "when Priscilla and Aquila heard him, they took him and expounded to him the way of God more accurately" (Acts 18:26). We see in 18:18 that "After this Paul stayed many days longer, and then took leave of the brethren and sailed for Syria, and with him Priscilla and Aquila." Paul, along with his friends and fellow tentmakers, is in Ephesus. After Paul left and went about strengthening the disciples in Galatia and Phrygia, we find Priscilla and Aquila still in Ephesus doing what they did in Corinth: working and going to the synagogue to preach. When this holy couple hear Apollos, a native of Alexandria, they recognize in him an affection for the faith, but one that it is lacking a bit. Were they being presumptuous in correcting Apollos? No! They had been roommates with the greatest evangelist in the known world! Carefully, they "expounded to him the way of God more accurately" (Acts 18:26). In a similar way, each of us has the chance to pass on what we have been given in the faith.

Practical Application

What does this passage say to you about your own life?

Many people have influenced us and helped us grow in the faith. What I love about this story is that Apollos doesn't wait or hold back from sharing in the synagogue, even though he knew only about the baptism of John while speaking accurately about Jesus. He did what he could with what he knew. Priscilla and Aquila don't deflate his passion; rather, they expound to him the way of God more accurately, which in turn means he will be even more effective. What they had received from Paul, they now passed on to Apollos.

You may not have everything figured out perfectly, but be encouraged. God will bring you people who can help you grow in your faith, and you will then pass on to others your insights. We often think mission work and evangelization are for priests and religious working in foreign lands, but you are called to share our faith right where we live! Be encouraged—you have a message. Maybe you are married and have been studying and reading about the faith for many years. Don't be afraid to reach out to the young and passionate, who may be a little unrefined in terms of content. Give what you have! I love the discipleship model we get from Paul. He evangelizes the world in which he lives and works, but he also models and disciples those with whom he lives and works—in this case Priscilla and Aquila. Keep in mind that Priscilla is very much part of this evangelization team. Not only do they witness and share the faith where they are at, but they disciple now Apollos. Why? Because this is the model of ministry they have grown up in. You and I have a message, and we have an audience. Let's get to work!

QUESTIONS

What is your message?

Who is your audience?

Is there someone you are discipling?

Thirty-First Meditation

*"This continued for two years, so that all the residents of
Asia heard the word of the Lord, both Jews and Greeks."*
— Acts 19:10

Catechetical Application

How can you encounter the Holy Spirit through this passage?

*What does it say about who the Holy Spirit is, what he does, and
the gifts he gives?*

Remember when the Holy Spirit prevented the disciples
from preaching in Asia? We can see now this had everything
to do with timing. Paul is now in Ephesus and he asks those
who were disciples, "Did you receive the Holy Spirit when you
believed?" Paul finds out that the answer is no. They have been
baptized into John's baptism, which was one of repentance. They
knew they needed to change and looked forward to this new
way of living, and Paul, realizing this, gives them what they
need. "On hearing this, they were baptized in the name of the
Lord Jesus. And when Paul had laid his hands upon them, the
Holy Spirit came on them; and they spoke with tongues and
prophesied. There were about twelve of them in all" (Acts 19:5-7).
When we read verse ten, it is amazing to note that from these
twelve the whole of Asia heard the word of the Lord, both Jew
and Greek. In many ways, this event is a bit of a microcosm of

the whole of Luke and Acts. We have a call to conversion and repentance. Paul, like John the Baptist, proclaims the Messiah, and many come to be disciples of Christ. They are baptized, and the Spirit falls upon them. These twelve, having been filled with the Spirit go, and witness.

We truly are a part of something great!

PRACTICAL APPLICATION

What does this passage say to you about your own life?

For all those times that you have held your tongue and been silent, know that there will be a time when you will be able to speak with clarity the beauty of your faith. The timing may be unknown to us, but when God works it is beautiful. The people who heard the message of Jesus from Paul were now ready to believe. They heard and responded with a desire for baptism. They were filled with the Spirit and spoke in tongues and prophesied. It was like a mini-Pentecost! They go and share the Gospel.

You have believed, been baptized, and filled with the Spirit. The timing for you to share is in God's hands. He is working with the people that you will meet and speak with. Let him do his work, and when the timing is right, your message, which is his message, will be received more fruitfully.

In many ways, the Acts of the Apostles gives us a sense of peace when it comes to evangelization. God is working through people in their regular circumstances to reach others of different cultures and beliefs. God knows the obstacles you will face. He knows you will be opposed spiritually and sometimes even physically. Let him bring you to where you need to be, to speak to those you are meant to reach. This is a great comfort to know that it is not up to you to make everything happen in and of your own accord. God is at work, even in you? Especially in you!

QUESTIONS

Is the timing right for you to share your faith?

When have you felt most comfortable sharing your faith?

Thirty-Second Meditation

"On the first day of the week, when we met to break bread, Paul was holding a discussion with them; since he intended to leave the next day, he continued speaking until midnight. There were many lamps in the room upstairs where we were meeting. A young man named Eutychus, who was sitting in the window, began to sink off into a deep sleep while Paul talked still longer. Overcome by sleep, he fell to the ground three floors below and was picked up dead. But Paul went down, and bending over him took him in his arms and said, 'Do not be alarmed, for his life is in him.' Then Paul went upstairs, and after he had broken bread and eaten, he continued to converse with them until dawn; then he left. Meanwhile they had taken the boy away alive and were not a little comforted."

— Acts 20:7-12

Catechetical Application

How can you encounter the Holy Spirit through this passage?

What does it say about who the Holy Spirit is, what he does, and the gifts he gives?

There are simply some passages of Acts that are amazing! Be encouraged if you get sleepy in Mass. You're not alone. Here is Eutychus, who gets to listen to the great St. Paul preach, and he falls asleep. Yes, it was late, with a dimly lit and crowded room, but still ... he is young, and this is Paul we are talking about. Not only does he fall asleep, he falls from the window and dies. As a speaker, I would be horrified and feel personally responsible if someone fell from a window at one of my talks and died! Paul, though, seems relaxed. He goes downstairs, says the boy's life is in him after falling three stories, holds him in his arms, and goes up to eat! Not only that, he continues to speak until dawn! Do you think anyone else fell asleep that night? Not likely! I absolutely love the last phrase about taking the boy away alive "and were not a little comforted."

PRACTICAL APPLICATION

What does this passage say to you about your own life?

What stands out about this story are several beautiful points. First, Paul wants to ensure that these people are prepared in their knowledge and understanding of the faith. He basically gives a mini-retreat that evening. The material and message matter. Sometimes, we can find ourselves a little frustrated at the "rules" we have had to learn about our faith over the years. Maybe you have many memories being bored in religious education classes as a young person. Those in teaching positions in the Church have a responsibility to articulate why we believe what we believe. Hearing and understanding what we believe and why is key. Second, we may not feel completely tuned in to the teachings of the Church every day. We are human. We get hungry and sleepy. This is normal! Third, notice how Paul comforts the people by telling them not to be alarmed. These are not empty words. If Paul had said that and left the boy unattended, continuing to preach, and at the conclusion the boy remained dead, the people would not have gone away comforted. Paul speaks these words, and they are followed by action. The boy is alive and well.

When we look at the Scriptures we can always glean something from the passages that are particularly interesting. I am confident that Eutychus told his story countless times for the rest of his life. Not many of us have that adventurous of a story when it comes to hearing the message of our faith, yet we are all brought to life by the words of God. In our own experience we have many moments of exhaustion, like the apostles in the Garden of Gethsemane. Listening to God's word, allowing it to touch our lives and awaken our hearts, is part of the Spirit's impact. I think Paul was calm because he knew that God was going to do something amazing, and that the work of the Spirit was greater than any accident and human weakness.

QUESTIONS

How difficult is it for you to focus on reading the Bible?

Do you wonder what ever happened to that young man?

Thirty-Third Meditation

*"And now, as a captive to the Spirit, I am on my way
to Jerusalem, not knowing what will happen to me there,
except that the Holy Spirit testifies to me in every city that
imprisonment and persecutions are waiting for me."*
— Acts 20:22,23

Catechetical Application

How can you encounter the Holy Spirit through this passage?

*What does it say about who the Holy Spirit is, what he does, and
the gifts he gives?*

I love these phrases: "captive to the Spirit," "the Holy Spirit
testifies to me." The relationship Paul has with the Holy Spirit is
so personal and intimate. He is on his way to Jerusalem, and it is
nothing but imprisonment and persecution that awaits. Would
you still go? He is aware of what God is asking of him, and
he nonetheless is willing to move forward. What comfort and
consolation the Holy Spirit gives, even amidst the difficulties we
face. In many ways, the saying, "Where God guides, he provides"
is applicable here. God is asking something total from St. Paul,
and Paul is willing to move forward in obedience. In fact, verse
24 says, "But I do not count my life of any value to myself, if only
I may finish my course and the ministry that I received from the
Lord Jesus, to testify to the good news of God's grace."

What Paul wants is to be completely given over to God. He received the message from Jesus, and he is prompted by the Holy Spirit to testify to the good news of God's grace. This is wonderfully Trinitarian. The Spirit of God is completely in harmony with God the Father and God the Son. The Holy Spirit is speaking to Paul and disclosing to him the reality of what is before him in this mission. The gift of God is not an avoidance of difficulty; rather, it is his presence and strength regardless the obstacle he may face. Paul is willing to endure all things. We need to ask if we too will be open to wherever God may lead, even if it isn't comfortable.

PRACTICAL APPLICATION

What does this passage say to you about your own life?

Some may say, "But Chris, St. Paul was called to be a missionary. He had an encounter with Christ, obviously knew the message of faith, wrote most of the New Testament, is on speaking terms with the Holy Spirit, and ends his life with great heroic virtue. He was a saint, and I am not." Well, keep this in mind, you too are called to share the faith wherever you may be. At work and at home, you are truly Jesus' hands and feet. You have had an encounter with Christ, an encounter that began at baptism and continues at every Mass, where you truly encounter Jesus. You didn't write the New Testament, but you can read and soak in its words every day. You and I should be on speaking terms with the Holy Spirit, since he is within each of us! While you have not reached the end of your life yet, can you not see the path upon which you are on and where it will end? If you are not happy with where you are going, then change directions. God is ready to empower you as you make your way to your own Jerusalem. Whether we encounter imprisonment or even death, know that God is with you. His Son is before you, and the Spirit is within.

QUESTIONS

Where are you heading?

How can you find peace knowing there is difficulty ahead?

THIRTY-FOURTH MEDITATION

"While we were staying for some days, a prophet named Agabus came down from Judea. And coming to us he took Paul's girdle and bound his own feet and hands and said, 'Thus says the Holy Spirit, "So shall the Jews at Jerusalem bind the man who owns this girdle and deliver him into the hands of the Gentiles."' When we heard this, we and the people there begged him not to go up to Jerusalem. Then Paul answered, 'What are you doing, weeping and breaking my heart? For I am ready not only to be imprisoned but even to die at Jerusalem for the name of the Lord Jesus.'"
                                        – Acts 21:10-13

CATECHETICAL APPLICATION

How can you encounter the Holy Spirit through this passage?

What does it say about who the Holy Spirit is, what he does, and the gifts he gives?

In this chapter, there is a lot of talk and examples surrounding the ministry of prophets. Earlier, we saw Paul entering Philip the evangelist's home. Philip had four unmarried daughters who prophesied. Paul and his company were in Philip's home for some days, and it is during this time that Agabus arrives. He takes Paul's girdle and shows him what will happen to its owner. That man will be bound by the Jews in Jerusalem and delivered into the hands of the Gentiles.

Let's remember a few things that should help. Luke is the author not only of the Gospel that bears his name but also the Acts of the Apostles. The same Spirit that descended upon Jesus affirming the Father's favor is the same Spirit that has descended upon the disciples. The healing ministry of Jesus in the Gospels is now continued in the missionary work of the apostles. Jesus is handed over to the Roman authorities by the Jewish leaders and crucified. Paul goes to Jerusalem, where he will be bound and handed over by the Jews into the hands of the Gentiles. It is no wonder that there is so much opposition to Paul's journey to Jerusalem: "When we heard this, we and the people there begged him not to go up to Jerusalem" (Acts 21:12). "And having sought out the disciples, we stayed there for seven days. Through the Spirit they told Paul not to go on to Jerusalem" (Acts 21:4). But, like Jesus, Paul will be obedient to where he knows he has been called to go. The people respond, "And when he would not be persuaded, we ceased and said, 'The will of the Lord be done'" (Acts 21:14). This reminds me of Jesus' words in the Garden of Gethsemane, where he declares his intention to do the Father's will.

The work of the Spirit that was present with Jesus in the Garden, demonstrated in his obedience to the Father, is now seen working in Paul, who is obedient to the will of Jesus. The Spirit of God prepared Paul to obediently accept this time of difficulty, imprisonment, and torture, and the same Spirit moved within the people to accept what and where God was leading their beloved friend and mentor.

PRACTICAL APPLICATION

What does this passage say to you about your own life?

This is a wonderful and encouraging passage for all of us, who are keenly aware of our mortality. Knowing that God's

Spirit is working within us can bring us comfort as we face our future, and can comfort our family and friends who care so much about us. If you have ever been with a loved one who is near the end of their earthly journey, you know that along with sorrow there is joy based on our faith in the resurrection. Knowing that we will one day be reunited is often the only consolation we can cling to in these difficult times. For Paul's friends, I am sure felt that their friend was leaving them too early. They loved him and were moved by his words and presence, and the idea that he would go through difficulties and even death in an unjust way seemed almost too much for them. The Spirit of God not only gave confidence and courage to Paul, but was also at work in his friends. I don't know what you are facing today, but I do know that God's Spirit is working in you and those who care for you. Do not lose heart!

I also think we can take another consolation from this passage of Scripture, and that is that our work in witnessing to Christ is not over until it is over. Think of the letters that Paul wrote while on his missionary journeys, often imprisoned, and usually in times of difficulty. How much we have been blessed by his faithfulness to God, even when it meant such difficulty for him. I think this is really the heart of a father. Paul cared for those he ministered to, and he wanted to give to them everything he could to enable their success amidst great opposition. As parents, we want our children to be prepared for the real world, and this desire becomes greater as we grow older and realize that we are not guaranteed any specific length of time to give to them what they may need. Trusting in the Spirit as we move towards our Jerusalem is a witness and consolation to each of us that God will care for those we leave behind. There may be a tendency to resign ourselves to the impending doom of cancer or dementia, yet God can be trusted in and our Lord glorified as we embrace our mortality with the Spirit's leading. What is your Jerusalem? What is your imprisonment and torture? You are a letter being written for family and friends in this time of misunderstanding and suffering. You are a book of instruction on how to face the final chapter in another's life. Be strong, be faithful, and know that He is with you.

Questions

What is your Jerusalem?

How is your life, empowered by the Spirit a witness to your family and friends?

Thirty-Fifth Meditation

"As Paul was about to be brought into the barracks, he said to the tribune, 'May I say something to you?' And he said, 'Do you know Greek?' Are you not the Egyptian, then, who recently stirred up a revolt and led the four thousand men of the Assassins out into the wilderness?"

– Acts 21:37,38

Catechetical Application

How can you encounter the Holy Spirit through this passage?

What does it say about who the Holy Spirit is, what he does, and the gifts he gives?

Could these people get any more confused? Good grief. First, Paul arrives in Jerusalem and sees James and the elders. They know he is about to be falsely accused, so they have him go with four men to purify himself and avoid those zealous for the law who would wish him harm. It doesn't work. The Jews from Asia stir up the crowd and grab Paul. They assumed that since Paul was with Trophimus the Ephesian that he had brought Trophimus into the Temple. The city is aroused, and many are trying to kill him. Seeing the tribune and soldiers, the people stop beating Paul. He is arrested and bound in chains, and it is then that he asks to speak.

Not only is Paul trying to appease those who were antagonistic towards him, but he is misunderstood and falsely accused by the Jews of doing something he did not do. He is nearly beaten to death and placed in chains. It is then that Paul tells his story. What I love about his testimony is that he admits that he is certainly guilty of many things, but none have to do with why he is in chains. Yet Christ is glorified in his testimony and misunderstandings. "So those who were about to examine him withdrew from him instantly; and the tribune was also afraid, for he realized that Paul was a Roman citizen and that he had bound him" (Acts 22:29).

PRACTICAL APPLICATION

What does this passage say to you about your own life?

We have all felt misunderstood and may even have memories of being falsely accused of something. Did you have a brother or sister that seemed to get away with everything? Maybe you were the one who took the punishment regularly for your sibling's disobedience. Paul is misunderstood and falsely accused even to the point of being beaten. Then the Roman official misunderstands who he is as well. Paul can't get a break, so he speaks on his own behalf. His message is his conversion story. It is what he knows best, and this is our encouragement. While we may be misunderstood and even falsely accused of many things, it is when we share our story that people begin to realize who we are may not be what they originally thought.

Like Jesus, Paul is falsely accused and misunderstood. Both are beaten (Acts 22:25) and are treated unjustly by Jew and Gentile alike. Sharing our story does not mean that we will be immune from misunderstanding or contempt. Paul and Jesus are both rejected by Jewish and Roman leaders. We may find ourselves in a similar situation, as many of the faithful who have gone before us.

Paul shared his story, and in it he described how he mercilessly and violently pursued those who followed Jesus. One of the phrases that stands out to me is, "I persecuted this Way to the death, binding and delivering to prison both men and women, as the high priest and the whole council of elders bear me witness" (Acts 22:4,5). Paul told his story, and it was authentic, honest, vulnerable and effective. You have a story to tell as well. So often I run into people who tell me that they would likely be in prison or dead had the Lord not come into their life.

A funny story I heard recently involves a person I have met a couple times. He is a tall and muscular guy, who looks like he could have played professional football. He often laughs and we leave it at that. Recently, I heard how a woman from his church came up to him, insisting that he looked familiar. She mentioned this a couple of times throughout the evening, and the man's wife finally asked her if she had ever been to a certain male strip club in a nearby city. Before this man's conversion, he was a male stripper! I think the lady was more embarrassed than the man in question. His story is radical, because the God that he serves is radical. We all have a past, but God's mercy allows for us to have a different future.

St. Paul is an example of how we should act when we find ourselves falsely accused or when we are persecuted: we should tell our story. Telling who we were and were we've been, and how Christ rescued us, may not deliver us from misunderstanding, but it certainly can be a catalyst for change and conversion to those oppressors.

QUESTIONS

Have you ever been misunderstood?

Have you ever been persecuted for the faith?

How can you share your story more with others?

THIRTY-SIXTH MEDITATION

"The following night the Lord stood by him and said, 'Take courage, for as you have testified about me at Jerusalem, so you must bear witness also at Rome.'"

– Acts 23:11

CATECHETICAL APPLICATION

How can you encounter the Holy Spirit through this passage?

What does it say about who the Holy Spirit is, what he does, and the gifts he gives?

Just when we need him the most, the Lord will speak to us. Not that his message to Paul was a declaration that his suffering would immediately stop. We begin to realize that not only will there be misunderstandings, but that there are Jews who swore an oath to not eat or drink until they kill Paul. They tell the chief priests and elders this, and not a word is said by these leaders to discourage this plot.

In this story, we hear about Paul's sister and nephew. "Now the son of Paul's sister heard of their ambush; so he went and entered the barracks and told Paul" (Acts 23:16). As these men plot Paul's demise, we realize it isn't simply a couple angry Jewish zealots. "But do not yield to them; for more than forty of their men lie in ambush for him, having bound themselves by an oath neither to eat nor drink till they have killed him; and now they are ready, waiting for the promise from you" (Acts 23:21). The tribune tells Paul's nephew to say nothing and then tells two centurions to ready two hundred soldiers and seventy horsemen, along with two hundred spearmen. They are to get a mount ready for Paul and take him to Felix the governor. A letter is written by the tribune, Claudius Lysias, to Felix, in which he says, "I found that he was accused about questions of their law, but charged with nothing deserving death or imprisonment" (Acts 23:29).

From one prison to another, with accusers following him as he is taken from one city to another, none of this is a surprise to Paul. Jesus himself told him that he would give witness not only in Jerusalem but also in Rome. We will all encounter a variety of difficulties in our lives. While it seems that Paul gets a second helping of crazy circumstances in which to live out his faith, we all have been told by Jesus that we will have a cross to carry as we follow him.

PRACTICAL APPLICATION

What does this passage say to you about your own life?

What is your cross? Whatever difficulties or physical adversities you face, know that we have all been called to count it all joy when we encounter various trials (James 1:12) and that we are considered blessed when we experience persecution for righteousness sake. While we are blessed to live in the United States, where we are able to worship freely, there are many examples of religious persecution, albeit more subtle than overt. We all know of places around the world where Christians are not only imprisoned but are tortured and killed. Whether it be physical or cultural antagonism towards our faith, we are called to witness our story of the love of Jesus Christ, even if we are falsely accused, imprisoned, beaten, or betrayed. Jesus will not leave us or forget us in our time of need.

We get a glimpse here into the heart of Paul's family and friends. They love him and don't want him to be hurt. They see how inclined religious leaders are to bring unrest and violence against one they know to be truthful and caring. Paul's nephew wants to warn Paul of the plot against him, and his friends try to steer Paul away from places where people will try to do him harm. But they understand that the conviction of their friend to share God's love is set.

What is your motivation to endure hardship? What is your motivation to keep sharing your story even though most who hear will not change their opinions? Paul had an encounter with Jesus Christ, and this made all the difference in how he viewed himself and others. The Holy Spirit, allowed him to love all people and that same Spirit is within you and me.

When I think about my twenty years of ministry, I realize two things. First, I regret things that I have done in my past and recognize that I have the rest of my life to establish a new legacy in which I will be remembered. Like most of you, I have said things to others that were hurtful, I used and was used, I was envious and jealous, angry and lustful, filled with pride and practiced slothful habits. I was (and am) a sinner. The miracle of our faith, though, is that Jesus allows for us to be born again through baptism and be filled to overflowing with the Spirit. We can go to confession and be healed and forgiven for our sins. We can be imprisoned by our sinful actions, but the faithfulness of Jesus to deliver us is evident in the sacrament of reconciliation. I am sure that Paul was vividly aware of his past, but he determined to have that past be so far removed from his present. The God he knew was a God of new beginnings. This is our God as well.

Second, we do not have to follow the world's idea of success. The relationship we are given with Jesus enables us to be the fullest expression of humanity that we are called to be. The paradox is evident: to give myself fully to Jesus does not minimize the reality of who I am; rather, it gives me the power to be fully authentic.

As we read the story of how the Spirit works in Acts, we can see that God is not done performing great miracles with average people in every type of circumstance. The work of the Spirit cannot be repressed. The irrepressibility of the Holy Spirit is a comfort to everyone who willingly chooses to follow Christ, to the utter bafflement of the world. When we allow the Holy Spirit to work in us, we become fully ourselves, and are truly unstoppable in our faith, regardless the conflicts and confrontations.

QUESTIONS

What is your motivation to live this faith? To endure hardship?

What is going to be your new legacy?

Thirty-Seventh Meditation

"'King Agrippa, do you believe the prophets? I know that you believe.' And Agrippa said to Paul, 'In a short time you think to make me a Christian!' And Paul said, 'Whether short or long, I would to God that not only you but also all who hear me this day might become such as I am—except for these chains.'"

– Acts 26:27-29

Catechetical Application

How can you encounter the Holy Spirit through this passage?

What does it say about who the Holy Spirit is, what he does, and the gifts he gives?

Paul has spent a lot of time in prison. He continues to be misunderstood, and the saying "out of sight, out of mind" is applicable here. Each time Paul gets the chance to share why he has been misunderstood, he uses the opportunity to preach the Gospel in the hope that people may believe and be as he is—except for the chains.

We read these lines at the end of the twenty-sixty chapter: "Then the king rose, and the governor and Bernice and those who were sitting with them; and when they had withdrawn, they said to one another, 'This man is doing nothing to deserve death or imprisonment.' And Agrippa said to Festus, 'This man could have been set free if he had not appealed to Caesar'" (Acts 26:30-32).

I am reminded of Jesus and the constant deferment of responsibility by those who opposed him. For example, Pilate's washing his hands and doing nothing to save Jesus, a man he knew was innocent, from being put to death, as well as the declaration that Paul could have been set free had he not appealed to Caesar. With all of this forgetting and fumbling of Paul's captors, God knows full well where Paul is and what he calls him to do.

Think about this for a moment. Paul is left in prison for years. "But when two years had elapsed, Felix was succeeded by Porches Festus; and desiring to do the Jews a favor, Felix left Paul in prison" (Acts 24:27). In verse nine of the 25th chapter we also read, "But Festus, wishing to do the Jews a favor, said to Paul, 'Do you wish to go up to Jerusalem, and there be tried on these charges before me?'" I wonder why Festus (and before him Felix) keep wanting to do the Jews a favor? If we go back to the twenty-fourth chapter and look at verse 24 we may see a clue: "After some days, Felix came with his wife Drusilla, who was a Jewess; and he sent for Paul and heard him speak upon faith in Christ Jesus." Felix had a Jewish wife, so he does the Jews a favor by keeping Paul in prison. Then Festus, two years later, decides to continue to favor the Jews.

Political maneuvering with different ethnic groups may seem unusual and trivial, but it is evident nonetheless. Felix kept Paul in prison and conversed with him regularly, "At the same time he hoped that money would be given him by Paul" (Acts 24:26). Bribery, family connections, and political upheavals all come into play in the life of Paul. But all this misunderstanding, conniving, and plotting were allowed by God, perhaps so that he could reach certain people with his message. God, then, is at work in the most complicated situations and circumstances.

Reading Paul's defense, we see a man who is longing for everyone who hears him to become followers of Jesus. Beautiful!

PRACTICAL APPLICATION

What does this passage say to you about your own life?

We keep coming back to the same story in these final chapters of Acts. It is the story of a man who was willing to follow Jesus even amidst religious and political turmoil. The Holy Spirit working and speaking through Paul will ascend to world leaders by the time the tale is done. Even those in high and lofty places need to hear the Gospel, here it is Paul who has the great opportunity to do so. What is he doing during these moments? He is preaching to those who visit him in confinement, and he is witnessing God's love in difficult situations—even when those meeting him are seeking to be bribed. We know Paul is writing letters to the faithful as he is being treated poorly.

You and I have today to encourage those who come into our lives. Maybe the difficulties you have experienced were for the sole purpose of witnessing to one person you meet. Possibly, you are working with people who want you to compromise your faith or are expecting you to commit a sinful action, but let St. Paul encourage you to remain steadfast in your faith. The practicality of these verses continues to bring us back to the truth that God is working in and through us to reach a world that still needs the Good News.

A couple years of imprisonment may have been necessary for Paul to preach the Gospel to King Agrippa. Would you be willing to wait in a place of imprisonment so that you could witness God's love to someone? It seems like a radical call, yet maybe God has you in your present circumstance so that a particular person could finally hear from you a message of hope. See if you can take advantage of this moment in life where your path somehow miraculously intersects with theirs. Who knows, maybe this moment was years in the making!

Questions

Who is your King Agrippa?

Can you find a way to encourage someone today? Who? How?

Thirty-Eighth Meditation

*"So, as they disagreed among themselves, they departed, after
Paul had made one statement: 'The Holy Spirit was right
in saying to your fathers through Isaiah the prophet.'"*

– Acts 28:25

Catechetical Application

How can you encounter the Holy Spirit through this passage?

*What does it say about who the Holy Spirit is, what he does, and
the gifts he gives?*

Leading up to this last chapter in Acts, we find Paul
on a ship where, of course, no one is listening to him. They
are shipwrecked, and had it not been for him befriending a
centurion, Paul would have been killed. He gets bit by a viper
and everyone assumes he will die. Of course, he doesn't. Then,
while on the island of Malta, Publius' father is sick with fever
and dysentery, and Paul places his hands upon him and heals
him.

Paul travels some more, and l loved this line, "Putting in at
Syracuse, we stayed there for three days" (Acts 28:11). I am living
now just north of Syracuse, the one in New York, and I believe
that God is willing to do great things here through people such
as me. Finally, Paul arrives in Rome. "And when we came into

Rome, Paul was allowed to stay by himself, with the soldier that guarded him" (Acts 28:16).

As the story of the early Church wraps up in the Acts of the Apostles, we have this phrase I've highlighted concerning the Holy Spirit. A few things that stand out to me are that Paul acknowledges that it is the Holy Spirit speaking to their fathers through Isaiah. Paul knows that God is at work in him, and the fact that "this people's heart has grown dull, and their ears are heavy of hearing, and their eyes they have closed" (Acts 28:27) is proof to St. Paul that the message of salvation being sent to the Gentiles is certain. "Let it be known to you then that this salvation of God has been sent to the Gentiles; they will listen" (Acts 28:28). I hope we continue to be those who will listen.

PRACTICAL APPLICATION

What does this passage say to you about your own life?

Be willing to rest with confidence in the Scriptures, knowing that they are inspired by God and are there for your salvation. The *Catechism of the Catholic Church* states that God is the primary author of Sacred Scripture. The story is written for our salvation, and recognizing that any variable that you face is one that he has been prepared for all along. Trust in the fact that what God has done before to ensure the Gospel is spread throughout the world, he continues to do so not only through priests and religious men and women but through married couples passionate about the faith like Pricilla and Aquilla—and through friends and relatives, such as Apollos and Paul's nephew. God is ready to reach everyone, and you have the chance, through the power of the Holy Spirit, to share your story with those within your reach. You may be asked to go into an area that seems peculiar to some, but suddenly becomes very real and applicable to where you now find yourself. Let God guide you and know he is providing not only the opportunities for you to witness his love, but he is bringing you people, sometimes years in the working, to share the story of how God touched your life. Do not be afraid. The confidence of the very Spirit of God is with you to give you a voice that will be heard, even if it seems all that results is antagonism and opposition.

QUESTIONS

Do you feel any more confident about sharing your story with others now than before you began this book?

Can you see the plan God has for you where you are now?

Who can stop you if God is working in and through you?

Thirty-Ninth Meditation

Selected Texts

1. Irrepressibility of the Spirit over Natural Barriers
   A. Language: 2:6-11
   B. Storms: 27:7-9,10, 14-20, 27:24

2. Irrepressibility of the Spirit over Physical Barriers
   A. Sickness/lameness: 3:6, 9:33,34, 14:8-10
   B. Jail: 4:3-20 5:18, 12:1-10
   C. Geographical distances—limited only by HS:16:6,7

3. Irrepressibility of the Spirit over Supernatural Barriers
   A. Devil: 10:38
   B. Simon the Magician: 8:9-24
   C. Sons of Sceva: 19:14,15
   D. Idolatry:14:12, 15-18

4. Irrepressibility of Spirit over Religious Differences
   A. Jews: at Antioch and Iconium, 13:50, 14:19-21
   B. Pharisees/Saducees: 4:1-3, 5:18-19, 7:51
   C. Sorcerers: 13:6-11, 16:16-18
   D. Synagogue of Freedmen 6:9-14

5. Irrepressibility of Spirit over Internal Differences
    A. Council of Jerusalem: 4:15
    B. Ananias and Sapphira: 5:3-10

CATECHETICAL APPLICATION

How can you encounter the Holy Spirit through this passage?

What does it say about who the Holy Spirit is, what he does, and the gifts he gives?

If you spend some time going through these five pillars regarding the irrepressible impact of the Spirit of God, you will begin to realize that, with that same Spirit living in you, there is nothing that you can't do. There is no obstacle or opposition that will be able to repress what God wishes to say through your willing heart.

There are many natural barriers the early Church encountered that could have hindered the proclamation of the Gospel, yet these seemingly insurmountable obstacles are hurdled. Language barriers are overcome, as are storms that threaten the life of God's chosen evangelist, Paul.

There are many physical barriers that the early Church encountered, yet the work of the Holy Spirit in and through them was not repressed. Sicknesses that would keep people down were healed by the power of the Spirit, and the imprisonment of many faith-filled people was of no account when the Spirit wished for them to move on. God was in control, and the message of the Gospel was spread far and wide. The only reason we see the early missionaries not go into a particular distant land was the leading of the Spirit. Nothing physical can repress the Holy Spirit in the Acts of the Apostles, and nothing physical can repress that same Spirit within you!

Nothing spiritual could repress the Spirit of God in the early Church. Neither Satan, magicians, or those sympathetic to another spirit could halt the proclamation of the Good News. The sons of Sceva, and even the misunderstanding of who these empowered missionaries were, could not stop the Spirit of God from working greatly in the lives of the Gentiles. That same Spirit of God is within you as you face spiritual obstacles.

In our day of greater religious tolerance, many have reduced belief down to subjective ethics, which is the belief that each of us creates our own moral code. A denial of objective truth and the embrace of relativism does not make such a code of ethics correct or permissible. The early Church faced much opposition from religious and secular authorities, but the Spirit of God could not be repressed. Neither the opposition of the Pharisees and Sadducees, Roman governors, or evil spirits could stop the proclamation of Jesus as Lord. Think of all the times Peter and Paul were plotted against, but nothing stopped the work of the Holy Spirit. That same Spirit of God is within you, granting you miraculous possibilities despite the opposing influences that surround you.

The Holy Spirit cannot even be repressed by the various internal differences found in Acts. Whether it was internal bickering by the missionaries regarding who would come with them, or the sin of Ananias and Sapphira, the Holy Spirit worked mightily. With the vital question of what to do about the inclusion of the Greeks, the deep concern addressed by the Church at the Council of Jerusalem, the many human conflicts that often derail businesses and even friendships and family are all subject to the work of the Spirit. That same Spirit of God is working in you as you encounter difficulties with family and friends.

PRACTICAL APPLICATION

What does this passage say to you about your own life?

Knowing that you are prepared by the Holy Spirit to move forward to do God's will, what could possibly hinder you from stepping out in faith with great expectations? Nothing physical, natural, or spiritual can come between you and the story of God's love. Knowing where your story fits in the grand scheme of salvation history is something you will grow to understand more and more, but you do not have to be an expert in theology to share what God has done for you. This personal message, shared with love and authentic excitement can be a catalyst for many to want change in their lives.

In the end, you have a choice to make: Will you allow the Holy Spirit to move in and through you? If yes, then there is nothing that can stop you. Will you allow the Holy Spirit more room in your life? Will you give to him the worry you have about physical obstacles? (Think of Moses and his stuttering. That was not a valid excuse to keep God from using Moses to lead his people.) Will you allow the Holy Spirit to work in you even though you face natural barriers? Know that Jesus will bless you and allow your brokenness to help many, just as he took the seemingly insignificant offering of fish and loaves and miraculously fed thousands.

Physical obstacles are nothing to the prodigal generosity of the Holy Spirit. Will you allow the Holy Spirit to move in your life, even though you find yourself struggling with many spiritual adversaries? Remember: God is with you! The Holy Spirit was not repressed in the early Church, and he will not be repressed in you if you allow him to move within you. The same Spirit we have seen at work in the Acts of the Apostles is the same indwelling you through baptism. Get to know the Spirit and get excited knowing that great things are about to happen with your permission. Give the Holy Spirit permission to be irrepressible.

QUESTION

Will you give the Holy Spirit permission to work great things in your life?

FORTIETH MEDITATION

I wanted to end this book with a simple truth: The Person and work of the Spirit cannot be reduced to a feeling or charismatic expression. This faith that we cherish and share is not presented to an exclusive few who have the financial capacity to join, nor is it a club for those initiated into a secret knowledge imparted to a select few. The impact of the Person and work of the Spirit is nothing short of miraculous, both in the early Church and in the Church today. You and I need the impact and strength of the Spirit in all aspects of our lives.

Really, a relationship with the Holy Spirit continually brings us back to the Church, so that we can be empowered and strengthened. For those wanting to regularly be filled, the Holy Spirit comes and gives us the courage to share our faith in the midst of opposition. He fills us whenever we receive Jesus in the Eucharist or the sacraments. The Holy Spirit brings us deeper into an understanding of God's love and the life of the Church, of which we are a part. Eucharistic people are people who recognize their need for the Holy Spirit. In fact, the Spirit of God is a gift from the Father for all of us who follow Jesus.

PRACTICAL APPLICATION

What does this passage say to you about your own life?

I was at Mass this past Sunday, and I was thinking about the power of the Holy Spirit. The Mass consists of two main parts: the Liturgy of the Word and the Liturgy of the Eucharist. As Catholics, we believe that the Word of God is found in written (Sacred Scripture) and oral (Sacred Tradition) forms, and in the Mass, we see both of these present in a variety of ways.

In the first part of the Mass, the Liturgy of the Word, we see the priest celebrant vested in a particular way to symbolize the importance of this moment, with the altar carefully prepared in adherence to the magnitude of the heavenly occasion. The intentionality of each vessel and article of clothing is a visible reminder of this sacred moment. We hear the Scriptures proclaimed and then "explained" in the words of the priest (or deacon) in the homily.

As we transition from the Liturgy of the Word, which presents us with the salvific work of God throughout history, we enter the Liturgy of the Eucharist. As the priest holds his hands over the gifts on the altar, the Holy Spirit is called down to make these gifts holy. This is called the *epiclesis*, and it is a profound moment. With the Words of Institution ("This is my body ... this is my blood ... do this in remembrance of me ..."), the miracle of transubstantiation occurs, when the Holy Spirit changes the substance of what is bread and wine into the body, blood, soul, and divinity of Jesus Christ. The Holy Spirit gives us the Son, which is the way Jesus intended all of us to be nourished by him as he established the memorial at the Last Supper.

In many ways, we are called to be like that ordinary bread and wine, placed in the hands of Jesus Christ, transformed by the Holy Spirit and changed by his power, so that we can go and feed the hungry hearts within our reach. We are called to be *eucharistic*, and this is a gift of the Holy Spirit. What is the miracle of the Spirit's presence in your life going to look like?

Think about this: As we hear the story of salvation in proclaimed in the Liturgy of the Word, we have a chance to tell our story to others. How did we arrive here? In what ways has God moved in our hearts? Telling our story assists others in being open to the power of the Holy Spirit. As we offer our smallness and our brokenness to Jesus, the Holy Spirit comes upon us and empowers us; he changes us. Every Mass is an opportunity to be fed by Jesus, through the gift of the Spirit, so that we can know the Father. We can be Jesus' hands and feet, filled with the Spirit, inviting people to know the love of God the Father. What a holy opportunity we have, and what a generous God to remind us of this at every Eucharist.

When we look at the impact of the Spirit coming down upon average men and women in the early story of our Church, we realize greatness is not predicated upon our ability to string together convincing arguments; rather, it is about an openness to his Spirit, which paradoxically, when submitted to, allows us to be fully ourselves. This is our opportunity.

QUESTIONS

How can the Spirit work in your life to nourish the lives of others?

What miracle do you need from the Holy Spirit?

CONCLUSION

My encouragement to you is to invite the Holy Spirit into each moment of your day. Whether you are single, married, or professed religious, you have a need for the love of the Holy Spirit in your life. There will never be a time when you are forced to submit to the Spirit's call, but he *will* be persistent. He will continually call you to a deeper walk with him, of that you can be sure. The call to live an authentic life is enabled by the Holy Spirit within us. We can endure any obstacle or difficulty with the strength and irrepressible gifts of the Holy Spirit. You have been set up for success, and all that awaits is your simple yes.

What will happen when you say yes to the Holy Spirit in your life? Well, quite frankly you will change the world. We have the chance to be like the Blessed Mother and willingly submit to the Spirit of God. Her humble submission brought Jesus into the world, and nothing has been the same since. When you and I open ourselves to the Holy Spirit, Christ is seen working through us. We become his hands and his feet, because, after all it is his Spirit moving through us.

Humanity has been redeemed by Jesus and is empowered and moved by the Spirit of God. The world awaits with expectation, even if it cannot fully articulate its need. Stand in opposition to misunderstandings about the Holy Spirit. As you give yourself over more intentionally to the movement of the Spirit, you will become more authentic in your humanity. Don't be afraid to give the Spirit more of you, because you will then be able to give more to those around you. We lack nothing in our universal call to holiness, so go and preach the Gospel with your words and deeds. We have seen the impact of the Spirit upon willing and open hearts in the Acts of the Apostles. You are a part of this story, and as you allow the Holy Spirit to move in and through you, lives will be changed.

So why do we need the Holy Spirit? Because we were made by Love, to be loved, so that we can share this Love with those we meet.